A FOREST OF DOORS

An Orphan's Quest

L. A. Muse

Published by
Innovo Publishing, LLC
www.innovopublishing.com
1-888-546-2111

Providing Full-Service Publishing Services for
Christian Authors, Artists & Organizations: Hardbacks, Paperbacks,
eBooks, Audiobooks, Music & Film

A FOREST OF DOORS
An Orphan's Quest
Copyright © 2013 L. A. Muse
All rights reserved.

Scripture is taken from the New King James Version of the Bible. Copyright © 1982 by
Thomas Nelson, Inc. Used by permission. All rights reserved.
Printed in the United States of America.

Library of Congress Control Number: 2013945308
ISBN 13: 978-1-61314-166-3

Cover Design & Interior Layout: Innovo Publishing, LLC

Printed in the United States of America
U.S. Printing History

First Edition: August 2013

This is my story.

I'm glad you're here.

It helps me to know I'm not alone anymore.

Dedicated to

Brian, Karen (Sissy), Robbie, Kelly, and the little girl I was. You are my inspiration. May we never again know what it means to feel alone.

With Appreciation

I still cry when I reach the end of this story. I will always remember the loving support I received from those who generously gave their time, talent, and emotional insight to connect with a little orphaned girl, a hand puppet, and a place called Carver Road. Their brilliantly orchestrated walk with me through the doors of my life allowed me to completely forgive, heal, and find peace. Thank you.

TABLE OF CONTENTS

PROLOGUE

Maine became beautiful to me when Mother died. Dread had obscured it as a cold fog from the Penobscot River. It lift Karen had called me a few months before and said, "Mother i doing well; she's dying. I'm not sure what you want to do with just thought I should let you know."

I felt a sense of dread, not from fear, but of opening. I knew instantly I had to make a call to released her and to create one last opportunity fo called immediately to check on her.

"Hi! This is Lynnann."

"Hello, my child. How are you?"

"I'm fine. I heard that you're sick."

"You know I've always had this lun on."

"Yes, I've heard that. If you don' , I'm going to call from time to time to check and see how doing."

"No, I don't mind; that will be fine said. The conversation ended abruptly.

I called her regularly to check o er. The calls were always brief, and awkward. On the last call, I knew she was dying. This was my last chance.

"Hello?" Silence. "Hello, this is Lynnann. How are you doing today?"

"I'm fine."

"Well, I just wanted to let you know that I don't have any hard feelings toward you, and I forgive you."

"You forgive me for what?"

"I don't know; I just felt like I should say that to you."

"Well, thank you, dear."

"I'll check in with you in a few days."

It was a beautiful fall day. I had been riding through the mountains on the back of my husband's Harley when the call came.

"Donna's gone," Sissy said.

"Gone? Where?"

"She's dead, Lynnann."

I felt a familiar, crippling, visceral pain. I was seven, she left me once more, no good-bye.

1

THE FALL

From the pictures I've seen, we were happiest in Orsay, France. I wish I could remember that time. My parents were a dashing, young military couple, and life was good. Father tells stories of country drives in his new Audi, visits to nearby Paris, and our farmer neighbors sharing their chickens for dinner to be served with the head on. His Louisiana roots made the language easy for him to learn. He smiles wistfully when he speaks of it now a half century later. My memories unfortunately began when it was horribly wrong.

I was born in Bangor, Maine, on February 21, 1959. I was the second of five children. My father was of French and Austrian descent, and my mother was of Irish descent. Father, Bob Sepcich, was in the air force. As soon as he could, he signed for boot camp at Lackland Air Force Base in August of 1955 to escape living with his mom, Mildred. Later, he was stationed at Dow AFB in Bangor, Maine.

While at Dow, he met Donna. Her brother Percy introduced them. Their first date was a drive with friends. They were an attractive couple and couldn't keep their hands off each other. They soon had their first encounter, as he put it. He was afraid that would lead to him becoming a father, so he went TDY (Temporary Duty Yonder) for three months to Greenland, and then another three weeks in Puerto Rico. Soon after, he attended six weeks in non-commissioned officer (NCO) school in upstate New York. That was the first sign he was a runner.

When he returned, Donna contacted him, and they started a relationship, conceived Brian, and married five months later. They married in Portsmouth, New Hampshire. My older brother, Brian, was born in May of 1957. When I arrived in February of 1959, we moved to Orsay. My younger sister Karen, who I call Sissy, was born there and survived despite being a two-pound, two-ounce preemie.

Father was a projectionist at the base theater. The photos of him at the time showed he had adopted a Hollywood style. In my first memories of Father, I found him to be very handsome, strong, and he had what it took to love and protect us. Though he was seldom around, a few memories of him linger.

Mother was a very tall woman with red hair and small, brown eyes. Her hair was always perfect. Her milky skin was washed with a splash of freckles. She looked elegant.

We returned to Dow AFB in Maine in 1962. Robbie and Kelly were born there. We soon discovered Mother was a problem. When Father learned he was to do a tour of duty in Vietnam in 1965, he took the precaution of moving us to Louisiana to be near his family so they could help. We arrived just as Hurricane Betsy was slamming the area. With this portent, we should have turned around immediately.

While Father was in Vietnam, we were fighting another war at home. Mother's abuse and neglect surfaced. She drank more and often left us alone at night. When she was there, she would be entertaining one of our many "uncles," as she called them. There were so many that Sissy and I thought all men were called uncles. They would come over and leave the next morning. I felt sadness and anger each time they would turn Father's picture over on its face while they spent the night with Mother.

On one occasion, a man came to pick up Mother, and they told us they were going to go out for bread and milk. Mother returned days later. *Wouldn't you know it?* I thought, *she forgot the bread and milk!*

At the ages of five and six, I found myself trying to be mother to the rest of my brothers and sisters. I was the oldest female and was given the responsibility of taking care of the younger ones,

From left to right: Brian, Lynnann, Kelly, Karen, and Robbie

as well as overseeing my older brother who Mother never thought could take care of himself.

We were living in Louisiana the first time Mother left us alone for days. I can still smell the urine-soaked bedding and laundry permeating those overcast days. The baby, Kelly, was still in diapers, and Brian and Sissy both had trouble with wetting the bed.

I remember being desperate enough to use the bathtub as a washtub to attempt to provide clean sheets and clothing for us. Somehow, I felt if we were clean, we would be safe. I could never quite get us clean, and we were never quite safe either.

At the age of eight, Brian was full of energy and anger trying to deal with our solitary life. Though I was given the responsibility of caring for all the children when Mother was gone, I had very little control over what my older brother did. Consequently, Brian crawled out of his bedroom window when I wasn't looking and found himself in a near-fatal accident. I can still hear the screeching tires outside. I threw open the front door to see Brian lying in the street covered in blood.

I was unable to make a sound; the shock of what had just happened overtook me. A truck had hit Brian! Terror gripped me. I quickly herded Sissy, Robbie, and Kelly into a bedroom closet.

11

After the screaming sirens stopped, I remember a knock on our front door and a man's voice calling for us. "Open the door!" Kelly was afraid of the dark and would not stay quiet. I finally opened the closet door to find a house full of police officers wandering through trying to find our parents. One police officer said he was going to take care of Brian and that he would be okay. He said he wanted to take us for some ice cream, but he never did. Adults in my life seemed to make it a habit of forget promises.

I overheard them ask each other how anyone could live in such filth with no food in the house. They kept asking where our parents were. I told them that Mother had gone to get milk and bread at the grocery store. The officers wanted to know how long she had been gone, and I just told them not very long. If Mother had only been gone a day or two, that would have been the truth to me. They told us we should just stay put until they returned.

I heard one of the officers say he was going to get an order to remove us from our home. After the ambulance had taken Brian to the hospital, and the police had left, I took Sissy, Robbie, and Kelly and we set out walking down the road away from the house. I remember wondering where to go and knowing that I was not going to let them take us away. We walked several miles and eventually came to Great-Uncle Ernest Billiot's house. He greeted us at the screen door, cursing our mother. He sat smoking angrily at the kitchen table and told us we were welcome to stay the night, or however long it took to find our mother.

Mother was later found at a local bar and returned to us at Uncle Ernest's house drunk and inconvenienced by the near death of her son. I hated to leave with her drunk, but I knew that someone had to look after my brothers and sisters. In the car, she screamed at me, saying I should have seen to it that Brian didn't crawl out of the window. "You are a very bad girl!" she yelled. "Now your father's family will have something to gossip about!"

Brian returned in a couple of days. He still bears a very frightening scar as a reminder. She rewarded us for our behavior by leaving us in the car night after night while she caroused at the local bars.

One night, Mother got into a violent fight with one of the men she brought home with her. He rushed out of the house and to his car. Mother shook us awake and pushed us into her car. She was so angry and out of control that she intended to run him down. We were frightened and crying as she accelerated and chased him. Soon we heard the sickening crunch of metal as she crashed into another car.

After the wreck, we all huddled together in the back seat. I recall the police officer asking her why she was speeding. She told him she was on her way to get bread and milk. The officer offered to take us to the store but Mother refused and simply took her speeding ticket and us.

We spent many cold nights waiting in the car outside of bars. I can still hear Kelly crying from hunger or a wet diaper. Robbie would be bouncing from one end of the car to the other, Sissy would be off in a corner sucking her thumb, and Brian would be cursing Mother for keeping us imprisoned in the car night after night. My primary thoughts were of getting Kelly to stop crying and somehow getting us cleaned up from the smell of urine. The best I could do was to settle for letting Kelly suck on my hand, and silently pray for Mother to come soon.

Not long after that, we got word that Father would be returning home from Vietnam. The day he was to come home, Mother got into a huge fight with one of her man friends. This seemed to have little effect on my anticipation of Father's return. I just knew that now we would be fed, clothed, and safe.

2

FATHER'S RETURN

Father served in Vietnam for one year on a helicopter recovering KIA (killed in action) soldiers. In 1966, he learned from his commanding officer that Mother was creating problems on base back home. Rumors were surfacing of us being neglected, a character named Mr. Boudreaux, the law, and counterfeiting. It became clear we were not being taken care of.

Father was discharged and returned to us in Westwego, LA. I was so very excited the night before he came home that I could hardly sleep. I got up in the middle of the night to see if Mother had returned home from her date. She had not, so I turned Father's picture back up and went back to bed in hopes of dreaming of his arrival in the morning.

The sun came in through my window and awoke me at dawn. We were all so excited about Father's return. We jumped up and down on the beds, laughed, and played. Mother still was not home. I really didn't care. Finally, around lunchtime, she pulled into the drive on the back of a man's motorcycle. My stomach hurt as I looked out at them from the front door.

When she came in the door, we were all clamoring about when Father would be arriving. I was always very cautious with Mother when she came in after being out all night. The drinking made her mean. Her angry reply to our questions was to say that Father's plane had been delayed, and he would be in around suppertime.

The boyfriend stayed most of the day. For the first time, Mother got a babysitter to care for us while she went to pick Father up that evening. She promised to be back shortly.

Hours crept by and again it was time for us to go to bed. Father did not appear at our door. The babysitter finally left, and again that lonely feeling set in.

Morning finally came, and I ran into the bedroom to find Mother fast asleep. Father was not in her bed. My heart sank, wondering where Father was. As I wandered into the living room, there he was asleep on the sofa. He awoke with five little faces all beaming with happiness, staring at him that morning.

Left to right: Brian, Father, Karen, and Lynnann

The happy occasion was short lived. They fought continuously for two weeks. Mother would hit him with her fists. She fought like a man and oftentimes, there was blood.

A police officer showed up after one of their fights and took Mother away to jail. Father was not the same man. He was sick of the dirty condition of the house and never having anything clean to wear. The smell of urine was always prevalent. That made him angry. His temper was very short with us too. I recall him pulling my hair and slapping my face. It wasn't long after his return he found out about Mother's indiscretions. He was so angry he just loaded everything up, and we moved.

The story we were told was that Father was taking us to Michigan to look for work. There were many violent fights on the way. Mother always had a can of beer in her hand, as did Father.

In Michigan, he left us. I remember him coming into our bedroom and waking us one night. He kissed us and gave us a hugs. As he headed for the door, I sat up and asked where he was going. He said to the store. He never came back.

I later found out he went straight to Western Union to pick up money wired by his mother and returned to Louisiana without us. He quickly got into a bar fight and signed himself into Charity Hospital to avoid jail for drunken disorder and assault. Mother took us to Maine to be closer to her family.

MOTHER AGAIN

For one month, we were in Mother's total care, or lack of it. Mother leased an apartment in Old Town, across the street from our grandparents' apartment. Our landlord, Mr. Goldsmith, owned many properties in the area, including the Goldsmith Department Store located at the bottom of Goldsmith Lane. We never went into the store.

Old Town is a small city in Penobscot County, Maine. The town's long history of logging and manufacturing left the Penobscot River heavily polluted; occasionally sludge covered the surface, giving little resemblance to a river. Our apartment sat between two old brick factories—the Old Town Canoe Company and Georgia Pacific Paper Mill. The pungent tang of a devil's brew of industrial liquids filled the air. It seemed a marshy, cursed place to me.

There, the previous pattern of neglect began all over again. Once again, I became the mother of my siblings, cleaning and caring for them the best I could. Night after night, I watched Mother put on her makeup to get ready for another night out.

On one such occasion, Mother returned in her usual drunken stupor, and I helped her into bed. The children slept in the next room. On this particular night, I awoke to the smell of something burning.

I ran into Mother's room and discovered her bed was on fire. She had fallen asleep with a cigarette in her mouth, and it had caught

17

the bedspread on fire. She screamed for me to get some water. I rushed to throw water on the bed to put out the fire. She just rolled over and fell back to sleep.

Later on, I found myself in trouble with the local grocery store owner. I had been sent to the store for some bread and milk, but we all had an uncontrollable urge for a piece of chewing gum. I decided to get the milk and help myself to four pieces of gum. I just didn't have the money to pay. The owner saw what I did and called my grandmother about the matter. She in turn told Mother. When Mother returned home, she took me back to the store and made me count out a hundred pieces of gum, one at a time, and we took them home.

That evening, she boiled lobster for herself and Mr. Boudreaux and made peanut butter sandwiches for us. She put the children to bed and kept me up so I could chew all one hundred pieces of gum before I went to bed. I still find cinnamon gum a bit repulsive. Lesson learned.

Mother came to the realization she no longer wanted us. Her story was that her parents had conspired to have us taken away. As I learned later, she signed papers on August 30, 1966, releasing us to the Bangor Children's Home. The children's home files state she blamed her children for her failed marriage. She did not even have the compassion to deliver us to the home herself.

Mother drove us to spend the night with Grammy and Grampy. Grammy was a homemaker who never learned to drive and was fearful of water. She was short and plump with neat silver hair back combed to add height. Her face was soft and round with red lips. To me, she looked like Mrs. Claus. Throughout his career, Grampy had been an accountant in Canada, a lumberjack, and a dispatcher for a taxi company on Goldsmith Lane. He was tall with a long, narrow nose ending in a sharp point. He was lean and defined under his plaid flannel shirts, dark pants, and heavy shoes.

The next day, Grammy brought out the big, metal washtub. We bathed there on the floor between the sink and stove. She had a fear one of us would drown, so she always kept us in sight. We dressed and sat on the couch in the living room.

My grandparents spoke in hushed voices in the kitchen. Grampy sat at the table slumped over a glass of vodka, cigarettes, and a full ashtray. He never moved. I had a sick feeling in my stomach as Grammy walked into the living room wearing her starched flower-print cotton dress. I smelled her perfumed powder. She stood in front of us, and I watched her bright red lips moving, barely hearing.

"Your mother is gone. She is not coming back, and you are going to go away."

"Where?" I asked.

"A home for children."

She turned to a knock at the door. Two women entered and led us down the stairs to the driveway. A car was parked with the back doors open, and we were instructed to get in. First Brian, and then Sissy stepped in. I turned to Grammy with tears streaming down my face, pleading, "Please don't make us go! We don't want to go! Grammy, I can help you. I can take care of us. We won't upset you; we will be good, please Grammy! I don't want to go!"

She stood silently crying. She hugged us and helped us into the car. Robbie and Kelly stayed with Grammy and Grampy. That was September 1, 1966.

3

ASYLUM

For 130 years, the Bangor Children's Home had terrified new arrivals. Originally, it was called the Bangor Female Orphan Asylum. The residents were called inmates then.

We rode there in silence in the back seat of the social worker's car. The social worker smelled beautiful. It was a perfect New England fall day. Sun and shadow played through the interior of the car as we turned into the long, circular drive. When we saw the building, Brian and I glanced nervously at each other over the top of Sissy's small head. It was a dark, brooding, three-story, Victorian Gothic horror perched at the top of a hill. To me, the orphanage seemed ready to pounce and swallow us through its massive wooden doors.

A man raking leaves by the entry stopped to watch us as we arrived; he was expressionless. I felt a stab of fear as the social worker opened the car doors and waited for us to get out. The groundskeeper watched silently nearby. I froze. I finally stepped out and turned to help Sissy, who didn't want to go. We held hands and walked slowly to the steps. I could smell the warm earthiness of the leaves and heard the rasp of the rake behind us as we started up the steps.

We waited at the door. A massive deadbolt turned and the door opened. We stepped inside and the door locked shut behind us. We followed the social worker to a large office on the left. Behind a dark desk was a very plain woman wearing a khaki dress and the thickest hose I had ever seen. She introduced herself as the head matron. She remained seated. She motioned for us to take seats in metal chairs across from her. My feet dangled from the chair, and Sissy's little legs stuck straight out.

"Are you Protestant or Catholic?"

"I don't know," I replied.

"Well, your father is a Catholic. If anyone asks you that question, tell them you are Catholic. Here you will do chores, and we have rules. If you do not follow the rules, you will have punishment. These ladies will show you where you will sleep."

Bangor Children's Home

We walked up three floors of massive stairs into a completely white room with no decorations at all. Beds lined the walls. It looked like eternity to me. We were directed to a bed where Floor Mother said, "Sissy, this is your bed; this is your box. In this box are your shoes, your undergarments, and your dress. You will need to keep it all neat and folded." She then took me further away, repeated her speech, pulled down the covers, and showed me how to make a bed. When it was time to go to lunch, we followed the other girls. Lunch was an assembly line that smelled of bleach and food. I still avoid cafeterias at all costs.

At lunch, Sissy kept saying, "I don't like it here." I said, "It will be okay. We are in the same room." After lunch, we were given our uniforms—a red plaid dress and red shoes. The shoes were no ruby slippers. They were clunky and you couldn't click the heels to go home. I didn't like them. I felt conspicuous and different. We were marked with scarlet so society would know we were orphans.

That evening we took our nighties from our box, showered,

and then brushed our hair. We crawled into our white iron beds between crisp white sheets under a white blanket in our white room. I remember thinking, *This feels like Grammy's bed because it has two sheets.* The bed was the only good part of the experience.

Breakfast was back in the cafeteria, and then we would leave for school. We'd play in a treeless playground and stare at the beautiful trees just over the fence. It was the same routine every day.

Brian was put on another floor, and I only saw him when we would have yard time. Yard time seemed to never last long enough. I remember looking out over the fence and seeing cars drive down the road in front of the orphanage. I longed for one of them to be my mother coming to get me out of this prison.

In the back of the orphanage was a huge water tower they called the Standpipe. It was even larger than the orphanage. They told us two children climbed onto the Standpipe, fell in, and drowned. I'm sure they just wanted us to stay away from it so we wouldn't be hurt, but that seemed a cruel way to get the point across.

The Standpipe always made me feel like my life was in danger. The play yard was filled with children at playtime. Brian, Sissy, and I would always search each other out and play together. I would push Sissy on the swings. Brian would push me. I would soar so high that I felt I could just fly over the fence and somehow escape this captivity.

Mother returned to get us October 4, 1966, seven months later. Once again, the five of us were back together in the Goldsmith Lane apartment, but not for long. We were reunited for twelve weeks this time. We were totally alone the last five weeks.

Mr. Boudreaux stayed with Mother. He was tall and thin with dark, olive skin. He had black eyes and the thickest, blackest long hair I had ever seen. He always wanted me to sit on his lap, but Mother would get angry with me if I got too close to him. She made sure to remind me of how bad a girl I was.

One day, Mother had a fight with Mr. Boudreaux over whether she would stay with us or go with him. She chose to go with him, and so they left. She told no one of her plans to leave, not even her parents. I knew that if anyone found out we were alone again, we would all be separated. The food finally ran out along with the clean clothes.

Brian just could not stay in the house, and I was afraid he would be seen. My grandparents eventually checked on us and found out we had been abandoned once more. The next day, we were split apart, never again to be raised together.

On July 26, 1967, our social worker, Miss Munce, reappeared and took Sissy and me down the now-familiar road to the orphanage. Sissy had broken her glasses and she blinked at the blurred landscape. I felt sick. Miss Munce broke the silence with the news that Brian went to a private home, and Kelly and Robbie would be adopted because they were so young.

This time, we were told we were going in a few days with the head matron, Miss Mullins, and the other children to spend two weeks at the beach. The resort, Sandy Point, had a long tradition of welcoming the orphans each year. This took a tiny bit of the sting out of the return, but not much. We had no idea what to expect.

We stayed in a cottage at the Hersey Retreat. We picked blueberries and, with our stained fingers, put them in small wicker baskets. We ate more than we kept.

We took a small day trip to Fort Knox. The Penobscot Narrows Bridge and the imposing fort frightened me. It looked like a prison. I was worried we might be left there.

Miss Mullins walked on the beach with me alone the first day and told me I could take off my stiff red shoes. For the first time, I felt sand and it was wonderful. She tried to talk to me. Her conversation was as stiff and uncomfortable as the shoes.

The best memory Sissy and I share was of an underwater tea party. We slipped into the water and sat cross-legged facing each other on the bottom. We pretended to be pouring tea and drinking from cups in the cool, clear water. Here, it was just us. We felt safe and together. We rose to the surface for gulps of air, laughing. We continued this ritual until we were called out of the water.

School was tough for me because I didn't feel like I fit in. Wearing the Little Red Riding Hood outfits didn't help. One day on the way to school, a German shepherd ran after Sissy and ended up pulling off one of her shoes. He ran off with it. When we got back to the orphanage, the floor matron was angry with us because we were fifteen minutes late and had lost Sissy's shoe. We both got whipped with a paddle. I was so furious that I raised my hand to try to stop her. I spent several hours locked in a dark room over that.

Months passed with no news from any of my family or relatives. Meanwhile, life went on at the orphanage. Every Saturday my chores were to clean three flights of stairs with a bowl of soapy water and a toothbrush. It took hours, and at seven years of age, the stairs seemed to never end.

At mealtime, we would line up and walk down all those stairs to the kitchen. We always ate everything on our plate. Sissy had problems finishing her meals because she could not see well and had trouble controlling her spoon.

Playtime was thirty minutes a day in our playroom on the first floor. I had a very special friend in the playroom. At the annual Christmas party for us at Dow AFB, Santa Claus handed me a package marked "for boy or girl." I tore open the box. When I first saw his face, my eyes lit up, and I fell in love. He was a Pinocchio hand puppet with the biggest smile on his face. He always seemed glad to see me. I treasured those thirty minutes a day because I could be with my friend Pinocchio. God knew how much I needed a friend, one who would accept me just the way I was and never found fault in me.

The story of Pinocchio was one I lived. It was as if he and I could come alive for thirty minutes a day when I was allowed to play with him. I entertained Sissy with puppet shows and made her laugh with me. This may have been my first glimpse of the loving, energetic, happy little girl who existed beneath the scars of abandonment and neglect.

I was a lucky girl to have a friend like Pinocchio. This little friend gave me incentive to behave the way they expected me to. If there was anything I hated, it was being separated from Sissy, and my smiling friend, Pinocchio. I would do anything in order to get my playtime with Pinocchio. I don't know what I would have done if I hadn't had him there to give me a reason to live.

Many couples would come and go, looking us over like they were shopping for property. We took extra care to dress for them. Once, Sissy and I were dressed as Dutch girls with wooden shoes. Sissy complained, "I don't want to do this." I said, as I always did to her protests, "I know." I remember my first line: "I am a little Dutch girl . . ."

The orphanage would occasionally host an open house. I would step into my red Sunday dress with a white collar and slip on my freshly polished red shoes. Our faces were so clean that our noses shined. I helped Sissy dress. "I don't like this," she said, while I smoothed her honey blond hair. We were led down the three flights of stairs into the lobby with the other children and instructed to only tell the visitors our name and our age. We did not drink the punch or eat the cookies. They were only for the visitors.

Once after an open house, we were called down to meet a couple who were potential foster parents. I'm not sure what my picture of the ideal parents was, but at first glance, these people did not meet my expectations. I was judging them against my beautiful parents.

Foster Mother was very short with brown hair curled tightly. Her eyes were blue and small with a nose too large for her small face. Her lips were taut when she introduced herself as Mrs. Lord.

Foster Father also was short with brown hair and sparkling blue eyes, but his face was kind and he smiled at us. He seemed to sense our fear. He leaned down to Sissy and me. I noticed his stiff, white, arthritic fingers. His blue uniform had an unfamiliar smell— probably a combination of the fire station and a print shop where he worked. I thought, *I like him*. I was determined to be the very best girl I could be that weekend because Sissy and I wanted to be a part of anyone's family who would have us.

Miss Kenney, our caseworker, made arrangements for our potential foster parents to pick us up for a visit. I was eager to go, but Sissy dreaded the change.

I was excited about leaving, and yet I discovered that my friend Pinocchio would not be leaving with me. I argued, "He was my Christmas present!" He was the only thing in the world I thought was truly mine, and now these people were taking him away from me too. He had become no less to me than Brian, Kelly, and Robbie were at the time. It was just as if I had to relive my experience of losing them all over again.

Through it all, my friend taught me to never stop smiling no matter what the circumstance. Pinocchio and I parted that day. I vowed to myself that I would return for him.

4

CARVER ROAD

On Friday June 14, 1968, Miss Kenney drove Sissy and me south from Bangor on Highway 1. It was a clear summer morning. We held hands in the back seat. I was grieving the loss of Pinocchio and worried about facing another strange door.

"Do you think they'll like us?" Sissy asked.

"They already do like us. They met us at the orphanage, and they invited us to spend the weekend."

"Okay."

"We have to be good. Follow me, stay close to me, and it's going to be okay. No matter what, we don't split up."

We turned left from the highway onto a tree-lined street. The green street sign read Carver Road. Sissy and I strained to see the houses ahead. The road was a narrow, straight, asphalt path that seemed to stretch ahead of us forever. Norfolk pines crowded the road. The houses were hidden.

We passed neat lawns with hedges. Apple trees and flowering shrubs drenched in the summer sun filled the front yards. Behind them, a thick, dark pine forest beckoned. I loved it. I was excited. Sissy and I looked at each other and smiled. *We could be happy here*, I thought.

Mr. Earl Carver named Carver Road. He bought the land and sold off pieces for development over the years. Eventually in the 1930s, he built a home and gas station on the main road. This was later converted to a home.

We turned left into a drive. The number twenty-four was clearly marked on the mailbox. The house was large and beautiful. The first thing we noticed was the octagonal shape of the main part of the house surrounded by a wide porch. The upstairs was grey and the lower floor was white.

Miss Mabel E. Holland had purchased ten acres in 1907. She was a teacher in Hampden, and sold lots to finance her dream home. A few years later, she built the house. She surrounded it with apple trees and lilacs. Her spirit still filled the place. The forest to the east dropped steeply into the Penobscot River.

Miss Kenney opened our car door. We slid out holding our paper sacks. Bruce, a tall, thin boy with swooping blond hair and bright blue eyes, took our sacks. He smiled and said energetically, "Welcome to the family! You're part of us now. I'm excited you girls are here, 'cause I'm a foster kid too." I liked him immediately.

Sissy and I took each other's hand and followed him into the kitchen. Foster Mother talked briefly to Miss Kenney and walked her to the door.

Foster Mom turned to us. "We're glad you're here. Let me show you where you will sleep. We apologize we haven't gotten your room put together yet, so we have bunk beds down here in the study."

Foster Mother and Father walked us to our room. On the way, they introduced us to our new siblings waiting in the dining room. I thought, *This is like the Brady Bunch—three girls and three boys. Mom and Dad make eight.*

Michael was four years older than I was. He was introduced as "our adopted son." His eyes were strikingly blue; I had never seen eyes that color before. *They are pretty*, I thought. Black hair framed his fair-skinned face. I knew we would be friends immediately. He reminded me of my lost Pinocchio.

"Beth is our own daughter."

She could be trouble for me, I thought. She looked like Foster Mother.

"This is Bruce Ogden. He is our foster son. You've met him.

This is Andrew. He is our own son." He was small and lanky. His arms and hands fidgeted and twisted in the air uncontrollably. I wondered what was wrong with him. He turned his head to the side and said, "Hi." He seemed sweet. I felt sorry for him. I wanted to protect him.

They showed us the house. The living room had a piano; I was immediately interested. The wood floors followed the contour of the room in an octagon.

Lynnann and Sissy's apple tree on Carver Road

When the tour was over, we ate lunch. Foster Mother prepared egg salad sandwiches and tomato soup. We then went outside with the children to explore. Michael, Sissy, Bruce, and I walked ahead. Beth and Andrew followed behind.

"That shed will be the clubhouse for boys only," said Michael.

"I'm coming in there too," I said.

A large apple tree begged me to climb it. "I'm going to climb that tree."

"You can't climb that," said Michael.

"Don't!" begged Sissy.

I climbed the tree and jumped down.

We walked up Carver Road. Michael told us the Shaw boys

lived in the blue house. We walked toward the Penobscot, and passed a swampy area by the Shaw house. Cattails covered the swamp.

"Let's show them polliwogs!" said Michael.

"What are polliwogs?" I asked.

"Come here. We'll show you. Close your eyes and put your hand out."

Bruce chuckled.

I closed my eyes and felt something wet and slimy in my hand. I screamed and threw a wad of polliwog eggs into the swamp.

"You can't tell Mom I did that to you," said Michael.

"I don't like the swamp. I want to leave. I won't tell on you."

Next, we walked into the woods. This was the first forest I had ever been in. It seemed enchanted. There were no paths. A blanket of pine needles covered the ground, making our steps quiet and soft. The pines smelled clean and sweet. The forest opened onto a huge, sand-colored hole in the ground.

"This is the sandpit," said Michael.

We walked around the steep edges. There was no way to the bottom, and that scared me.

"These are blackberries," said Bruce. "You can eat them."

"I'm not trying them." After the polliwogs, trust would have to be rebuilt.

The blackberries were so thick we couldn't get to the river, but we could see it.

"The river is polluted," said Michael. "You can't swim in it. That old house over there is Old Man Keller's. He is mean and yells at us. You never want to go onto his property."

That Sunday was Father's Day. At church, Foster Father won the award for the most children—six kids. He stood up and testified jovially how grateful he was to have two new children added to his family on Father's Day. I was confused but hopeful this label was better than orphan. I didn't know what "foster child" meant, but I was ready for an adventure. Sissy was upset because we had heard Foster Father reassuring his biological daughter that she was still the princess. Sissy didn't like her.

After church, we returned to Carver Road. I took off the red dress for the last time and changed into play clothes. We all held hands at the lunch table. Foster Father prayed, thanking God for Sissy and me. When I heard that, I felt reassured that we would return later in the week. Everyone took turns praying. Sissy and I sat silently. The family drove us back to the orphanage. Foster Mother and Father checked us in. I overheard Foster Mother say, "We enjoyed the visit with the girls."

"We'll see you girls soon," Foster Father said.

They waved and left.

We sat on the edge of Sissy's bed. I was excited.

"I don't want to go," Sissy said.

"We need to be in a family. I liked them. It will be okay; we will be together." We talked about the weekend for a while and gradually fell asleep.

On June 20, 1968, Sissy and I were released to go with our new family. Miss Kenney arrived at the orphanage. We packed the remainder of our things in sacks and made the last trip down the staircase. It was cloudy. We were silent on the ride except our short answers to Miss Kenney's questions about our visit.

"You girls are really lucky. This is a good family," she said, turning onto Carver Road. We strained to see ahead. It was just as we remembered. Foster Mother welcomed us at the door. We had been freed from the orphanage.

"You can call me Mom or Mrs. Lord. You know where to put your things. Go put them away, girls." She returned to the kitchen to make lunch. *Well, I'm not calling you Mom*, I thought. The children followed us upstairs and watched curiously as we put our things away. We all returned to the kitchen.

"Do you like Miracle Whip or mustard on your potted meat sandwich?" she asked.

"I don't know." No one had ever given me a choice of what I would eat before. I was lost.

"Well then, I'll give you both and you can decide what you like." I still like both together.

When Foster Father came home from work that evening, we sat down to a dinner of chuck steak, mashed potatoes, and a wonderful bread pudding. We all held hands while Foster Father prayed. "Dear Heavenly Father," he began. His prayer was long—they were always long—and he ended with, "We ask these things in your Son Jesus' name. Amen."

The children started to pray in order. I was terrified. Fortunately, they skipped us this time. After dinner, we all had Bible study.

The summer of 1968 was full of new introductions. The six of us loaded up one morning in the blue, wood-paneled station wagon to go to Nana's. Michael sat in the front next to Foster Mother. He called "Shotgun!" first. Sissy and I rode in the back seat with Beth. Andrew and Bruce rode in the jump seats in back.

"We are going to see my mother. Call her Nana," Foster Mother said. "She is sick and in bed, so don't stand too close to her and be quite. Lynnann, Karen, you girls wait in the kitchen until I come get you. Beth and Andrew will see her first, then Michael and Bruce."

"Again, welcome to the family," said Michael as he tilted his head back and raised his eyebrows. Something about the way he said it made me feel sick. I grabbed Sissy's hand.

Foster Mother made a stop at Shaw's grocery store. She stepped into the store like a sergeant with his troops. She waved a list and coupons in her hand and barked orders. "Michael, go get milk. Bruce, pick out some Kool-Aid. Andrew and Beth, pick out two boxes of cereal."

Sissy and I stayed close to her as she pushed the cart rapidly. We watched in awe as she raked bread, sugar, chicken, chuck steak, and things we'd never seen into her rapidly filling cart. We were in and out and pulling into Nana's driveway in fifteen minutes. *Finally, an adult who actually gets bread and milk!* I thought.

Foster Mother ordered us out of the car and grabbed a bag of groceries. She fast-walked to the door, and opened it with her key. The house was white, not clean white, dirty white. The kitchen was small for a house so big, but it was clean and tidy. Beth and Andrew escaped down a hall. Foster Mother put away the groceries and disappeared after Beth and Andrew, pulling Michael and Bruce along.

I heard whispers and it reminded me of the day we were taken from Grammy's house. My stomach began to churn. I reached for Sissy's hand and froze. Foster Mother walked into the kitchen. I tried to read her expression. It gave me no clues. She motioned with her hand, "Girls, come." We followed her into the parlor. A woman was lying in a chaise lounge by the bay window. She was bigger than Foster Mother with thin, grey hair pulled tightly into a small bun on her neck.

"This is Lynnann and Karen, the two girls we took in from Bangor Children's Home. They are our foster daughters now."

Nana did not look at us. She stared out the bay window and said, "You have a daughter, Eleanor. You don't need any more children. Why do you and Raymond take these kinds of children into your home? I want to see Beth."

Foster Mother led us through another passage into a living room. The other children were sitting on the couch. They had heard; I could tell by looking at Michael's face. Our eyes met and I recognized the pain. Beth stood up with a smile on her face and followed her mother into the parlor.

The house was musty and damp. We sat quietly staring at the old photos and white doilies on end tables and waited.

Sissy and I did not have to see that Nana much after that incident. Foster Mother spared us. A few years later, Nana died. It was my first funeral. I did not cry.

Sissy and I met Foster Mother's sister Aunt Evie next. She was Foster Mother's identical twin. Aunt Evie was a nurse at the very hospital where I was born—Eastern Maine Medical Center. Aunt Evie was kind to us. She was unmarried and childless. I was impressed by her independence and her white uniform and hat. I had not met anyone like her before. I decided I wanted to be a nurse when I grew up. I took a course four years later and became a candy striper. Aunt Evie was pleased.

Sissy and I also met Foster Mom's older sister Alice. I was told she was not well, so we did not see her much. We met Aunt Alice's daughter Sandra and her husband, Dick. They had two little children, Ricky and Stephanie. Four years later, I babysat for Sandra. I would ride the bike Sissy and I shared up Carver Road turning right on Maine Street to Old County Road where Sandra lived.

That first summer, we took a road trip to Richmond, Maine, to visit with Grammy Lord, Aunt Shirley, and Uncle Linwood. They were Foster Dad's family. We stopped at Camp Wakonda along the way. This was my first time camping out in a tent with a sleeping bag. The tent was big. As soon as Michael and Dad finished putting it up, I walked through the zipped screen doorway to explore.

Two pieces of canvas divided the tent into three rooms. Sissy and I now had our very own piece of luggage—a psychedelic purple overnight bag we shared. I carried it to the girls' room in the tent and rolled out our sleeping bags. I zipped our sleeping bags together so we wouldn't be separated. We ate hot dogs washed down with lemon-lime Kool-Aid.

Later that evening, we roasted marshmallows on sticks. Foster Dad taught me how to roast the perfect marshmallows. "The trick is to keep turning the stick," he said. After a couple of really crispy black marshmallows, I had it down. I offered to roast everyone's marshmallows, and they let me.

Later that evening when the summer sun had disappeared into the night, Foster Dad called out "Lynnann! Karen! Have you girls ever seen the stars from outside before?" We scurried out the unzipped door. We lay on our backs on the picnic table looking up into the black sky. I saw the immense sparkle of stars. "Look at that moon, girls. Ever see a moon like that before?"

"I have seen the moon before," Sissy said.

"Not like this!" I said. I gazed up past the tall pine trees into the deep blue of the night, breathing in the hickory scent of our campfire and feeling a stir of butterflies in my tummy.

"You girls come in when you're ready," Foster Dad said, disappearing into the tent. I reached for Sissy's hand, and we lay looking without a word.

Michael walked by. "You two girls going somewhere?"

I replied, "To the moon." We giggled our way into the tent. This was my first of many family camping trips.

Along the way to Richmond, we counted license plates, slugged each other when we saw Volkswagen Beetles, and played I Spy. We arrived singing, "The Wheels on the Bus." Sissy and I began to feel a part of a real family.

Grammy Lord met us at the door. She was a short, square lady. Her kind blue eyes contrasted her worn face. She wore a faded cotton sundress. Her slippers shuffled on the tile as she walked quickly toward us. She welcomed us kindly, her stiff, bony hands reaching for us. Uncle Linwood was at the kitchen table and nodded as we walked by. He was very quiet. Aunt Shirley hurried toward us from a back room with her hands full of six coloring books and crayon sets. She peppered us with questions.

We took our coloring book and sat underneath the enchanting weeping willow tree just outside the door. "How old are you girls?" she asked.

"Sissy is seven; I'm nine."

"What grade are you in?"

"Sissy is in first; I'm in third."

"Where are your real mom and dad?"

I hesitated. Michael stepped in, "They have the same parents, Aunt Shirley."

"Where did you two girls come from?" she continued.

"Sissy came from France, and I came from Bangor."

Michael cut in again, "Aunt Shirley, you ask too many questions."

I thought of the mysterious weeping willow we passed

on the way to the door. Its thin branches swept the ground and created a secret play place where we could escape. I took Sissy's hand and walked to find Foster Mother in the kitchen. "May we have permission to play under the weeper?"

"Yes, go play."

We parted the branches like a tent door and stepped inside.

The tree became our escape during our future visits. We always found a special tree to talk secretly about the big things. At the house on Carver Road, it was a large, old apple tree. We hung like fruit in its branches. When we made agreements there, they were sealed with a pinky swear.

On the way home, we were trying to decide how to address our foster parents. We decided to wait until we could talk alone in the apple tree.

That evening on our way to bed, I kissed our foster parents on the cheek and said, "Good night."

I heard Sissy say, "Good night, Mom."

In our room I asked Sissy, "Why did you call her Mom?"

"I wanted to. Are you mad?"

"Nope."

"Sure?"

"Yes." I was not mad at all. I felt a small twinge of pain at the thought that Sissy might love her more than me. I don't recall when I started calling them Mom and Dad. It just seemed to happen.

Our first summer was packed with road trips. Mom and Dad made sure they educated us on Maine's rich history during the long drives. One beautiful day, Mom said, "We are going to Dorothea Dix Park for a picnic." The park was located in Hampden only fifteen minutes away.

Another day, we traveled to Fort Knox. The old fort beckoned us to explore. The dark, damp corridors led to small, musty rooms leading to deeper, smaller rooms. Michael sprinted ahead to jump out and scare us. Dad and Andrew walked to the canons pointing to the Penobscot River.

Bar Harbor was my favorite day trip. Many times during the years on Carver Road, we explored the trail around Jordan's pond. Small bridges led to adventure in the deep forests of clean-smelling pines. Wild flowers scented the air. We danced across rocks and skipped stones on the pond. Birds, butterflies, and cotton clouds decorated the pure air.

Further up the harbor, Thunder Hole spouted water forty feet in the air with a crash, the water washing down over the rock, trailing seaweed. Dad would then drive us along the steep, winding road up Cadillac Mountain. The steep drops frightened us. The view of the ocean through the pines and the feel of the wind in my hair as I poked my head through the open windows made me free, at last.

Our foster parents were very religious. They did their best to measure up to the standards of their church. We lived a very structured and rigid existence. Our new family was tough, but there for us. I loved having someone to call my family. Most importantly, they built a spiritual foundation that became a basis for my own belief.

As I grew, I began to feel an inexplicable urge to rebel. I found it difficult to fit in. I discovered there was a difference in the way a biological child and a foster child were treated. There even seemed to be a difference between an adopted child and a foster child. It was difficult to understand the set of standards I was to live by.

Mom was a strong, determined woman who paid her own way to college and graduated with a master's degree in education. I have few memories of tender moments, hugs, kisses, or a warm touch from her—I thought those things were love. I didn't know her actions and her work for us were her way of showing us she loved us. I stayed in trouble on a regular basis. I was not as willing to conform to this set of rules and regulations as most of the rest of the children were.

Often when I was irreverent toward Mom, I would be disciplined with her hairbrush on the back of my hands. Our relationship always felt strained. I never knew why until I learned years later that she had really just wanted Sissy, but agreed to take me only because the state of Maine refused to split Sissy and me up. Perhaps I sensed that. Perhaps I simply saw her as competition for Sissy's love. After all, I was Sissy's mother before she entered the picture. Whatever it was, my heart rebelled. I finally believed what everyone had told me—I was simply a "bad girl."

Sissy and I took baths with bath beads in a claw-foot bathtub. I accidentally popped a bead in her eye. She had already had three surgeries on her eyes. I jumped out to get Mom, but Sissy said, "No, no! You'll get in trouble." I felt terrible.

On Saturday night, the family would watch the TV show *Emergency!*, and then everyone else went to bed and I watched *Colombo* alone with Mom. I pin-curled her hair every Saturday night and combed out her hair on Sunday morning before church. I would always wait anxiously for her approval. Sometimes she would say, "That looks very nice, thank you." Sometimes she would just say "Thank you."

I often thought about my siblings. *Where are my babies, Kelly and Robbie? What happened to Brian?* I also found myself missing my friend Pinocchio. I had difficulty sleeping and constantly had to go to the restroom. I got in a lot of trouble for going to the bathroom too often during the night. I never lost my fear of being sent back to the orphanage.

School was tough because I found it hard to blend in. I always dreamed of just being a normal little girl, from a normal little town, who had a normal little family. Why couldn't I be normal? As I matured, I discovered extraordinary people are created from extraordinary circumstances.

I looked forward to the afternoons after school. We did our homework, practiced the piano for thirty minutes, and then played. My fondest memories are of playing with my big foster brother Michael.

Michael and I always seemed to have a special bond between us, which to this day has never been broken. I loved climbing the apple tree and having Michael teach me how to play basketball.

Michael enjoyed playing the guitar and singing, so I found that to be one of my favorite pastimes as well. He was my protector and friend. Michael made my experience in the foster home a very good one. He seemed, more than anyone else, willing to accept me just the way I was.

God has always made certain I had someone in my life close by to remind me I was a very special creation with or without a family. Michael was that person for me in the house on Carver Road.

We got up early, threw newspapers together, and grew to defend each other when the occasion presented itself. Defending each other even extended to our playtime. Michael would often play the part of Perry Mason. I was usually the one on trial, while the other children were the jury. Michael would always speak his mind and in this family that was always an opportunity to get into trouble. I believe Michael became very much my live Pinocchio. I never minded doing Michael's share of the ironing.

Our family life was perfectly normal. Mom would take us to the library each week where I read my way through the Hardy Boys and Nancy Drew mysteries. I was always lost in an adventure when Mom interrupted with, "Girls, time to set the table!" Birthdays were celebrated with our favorite meal and cake—carrot cake for Sissy and strawberry for me. We took horse-riding lessons. I reassured Sissy and gagged while cleaning hooves.

Christmastime was a predictable event each year. Each of us would get two presents wrapped in the funny papers. The holidays seemed to have little effect on Mom when it came to exhibiting a Christmas spirit. Dad, however, was a man with the capacity for warmth and genuine love, and every now and then, he would sneak us a hug or kiss. Before he died, I found he had also been left for a time in the Bangor Children's Home.

We formed our first long-term friendships on Carver Road. The Shaw family lived across the street in the blue house. The family was of strong Scottish descent with four sons. Mrs. Shaw was an attractive, tall, elegant lady with perfect hair. She always seemed to be backing out of the driveway to go to one of her several jobs. Her voice was sweet and soft but commanding when she lined out her four boys. Mr. Shaw had black hair with a perfect wave slicked smartly back.

The Shaw boys were David, Danny, Dana, and Dean. The first time we met them was the first of many times we talked about boys in our apple tree. They attended our church and walked with us to the bus stop. David and Danny had warm, soft brown eyes. Danny's skin was olive. His light brown hair swooped carelessly over his eyes. David's skin tone was lighter with darker hair. Dana had the most beautiful green eyes I had ever seen; they looked like green marbles. His hair was brown above his freckled face. Dean was the youngest, with green eyes and black hair.

The Shaws were all musically gifted. They sang in church. Mrs. Shaw would sing the solo parts in her beautifully high, clear voice. David played the trumpet. Dan played the trombone. Dana played the saxophone. I wondered how one family could have so much talent. The Shaw boys also excelled at sports. David played football and baseball, Danny played football. Dana played football, baseball, and basketball, and Dean was a sports manager.

Sissy and I talked about the boys in our apple tree; I liked Danny and she liked Dana. We were so sad when they ended up moving. I would still see them at church, but it was never quite the same.

The Harvey family moved into the Shaws' house. They had four girls: Cathy, Lori, Vicky, and Christie. The Harvey family also went to our church. I became good friends with Cathy and Lori. Like the Shaws, this family was musically gifted also. The Harvey girls would sing quartets in church. I began to believe the blue house had the power to give people musical talent.

Just before the evening meal, I would often wander through the woods near our house picking berries and enjoying the quiet time alone. Mom would ring a loud bell, which could be heard by everyone in the area, when dinner was ready. She expected us to come running when we heard it ring.

One day I was walking through the woods around the sandpit. I heard my name being called in a hushed sort of way. Something about it scared me, and I started to run for the house. Before I took very many steps, a man's hand grabbed me by the arm. I turned and recognized a man I had seen at my school. I explained that the dinner bell was about to ring, and I was in a hurry to get home for dinner. He told me that my parents would be just fine and that I was going to stay and spend a little time with him. After, he told me if I said anything about what had happened that I would be sent back to the orphanage. He seemed to know my greatest fear. I heard the dinner bell ring, and I knew I would be in trouble if I didn't respond to it immediately.

When I got home, Mom asked me if I had heard the bell. She thought I had been playing with the neighborhood boys. She was furious with me because dinner was over and the other children were cleaning up. I told her I tried to get away but couldn't. She slapped my face, grounded me, and sent me to bed. I asked if I could take a bath and she shouted, "No! Are you dirty?" I replied, "Yes, very dirty." She then mumbled that if I didn't play with the neighborhood boys so much, I wouldn't get so dirty.

I went to bed that night feeling so hurt and confused, with plenty of reassurance that I was a very bad girl. I was actually happy to be grounded. I felt like that was the best way for me to be safe.

I was forced to deal with this person at school daily. I avoided any direct eye contact, and always turned my head whenever we would pass in the halls or outside the building.

Months passed before I had another encounter with this man, and this time it was much the same as the first time, except there was much more force. It was as if he simply hated me. After that, I would never go anywhere alone, or even leave my front porch alone. I always seemed to figure out a way to be grounded after that. Consciously or subconsciously, it was a solution to the problem.

It took years to realize I had been sexually molested on those late afternoons. I was unable to remember the event until my foster brother Michael asked me about it when I was thirty-four years old. He asked if I'd ever had an encounter with a man at the school who had recently been accused of molesting children over a long period of time. I had blocked it out completely until Mom reminded me almost twenty-seven years later that she should have listened to me when I tried to tell her that a man from the school had kept me from being on time for dinner one night.

Summer came and went and my first year of junior high began. I felt safe because I had a new best friend, Ginny. She was tall with a stylish blond bob hairstyle and blue eyes. We were together all the time in school. I really wanted Ginny to like me so I didn't talk much about my past. I never mentioned what had happened to me during the summer in the sandpit. I didn't want her to think I was a bad girl. One day at school the man from the sandpit caught me in the hallway after I had gone to the restroom. I was alone with him again, and again his hands were all over me.

He heard someone's voice coming down the hall and immediately left me standing there. When I finally returned to my classroom, Ginny could see that I was upset. She kept asking what was wrong. Eventually, I broke down and told her what had happened. Ginny insisted that I tell my foster parents. She always helped me feel stronger when I struggled with self-doubt and insecurity.

That day after school on the way out to the bus, I saw the man and I told him I was going to tell my foster parents what he'd done. I ran to the bus as soon as I said it and went all the way to the back of the bus to sit.

I felt so good and was grateful for Ginny's little push to confront this man. I did try to tell Mom when I got home, but she would not believe me. I decided to drop it. I was resigned to the fact that she was right; I was a very bad girl. I blocked it all out of my mind and focused on my friendship with Ginny at school and my relationship with Sissy and Michael at home.

The man at school never bothered me again. I continued

to avoid him at all costs. Ginny and I had some good times but my foster parents didn't like her much, and her parents didn't like me very much either. We held onto each other anyway, all the way through junior high.

Michael graduated from high school and left for college. We drove him to Boston. We spent the night in a tent at a campground on that trip. I recall burning myself roasting a marshmallow. The pain from the burn was nothing compared to what I felt in my heart. I have never been able to say goodbye to someone I love with any dignity. I now understand why.

Michael was my friend, my big brother, my defender, my short-nosed Pinocchio. How would I survive without him? We always stood on common ground and knew how each other felt while growing up.

When we unloaded his luggage and took it to his room, I just could not bear to leave. I eventually did, but not without being overwhelmed with tears. I felt those old feelings of abandonment again. Mikey was gone. From the age of fourteen to the age of thirty-three, I lived without seeing my special friend again.

After Michael left, I just couldn't find any sense of direction or purpose in anything I did other than taking care of Sissy. My foster parents seemed to really keep a tight rein on me and always felt a need to ground me for anything they were disappointed in. To add to the confusion, Mother reappeared after seven years of being totally out of our lives. I had learned to survive for seven years without her, and then she decided to come back.

She called occasionally and even sent some gifts to Sissy and me. I called them guilt gifts. It was a brilliant strategy on her part. If anything could motivate me, it was the feeling of being guilty for something. She confused me with her use of the word *love* and talk of wanting and needing me, all of this right before she would leave again. I wanted to believe her in the worst way, but when I asked her if I could please come and live with her, she said it just wasn't time yet. I really began to resent and hate her all over again. With every passing holiday and broken promise to visit us that came along, I came to the realization that I was much better off without her in my life.

When I asked her about Brian, Robbie, and Kelly, she would always tell me that her parents conspired to take us away from her. She said she thought we were with her parents.

It was around this time when I asked Jesus to come into my life. My decision was based on my very real fear of ending up in hell, rather than because I loved Him. I was sure a person as awful as I was would surely go to hell if something happened and I died prematurely. My foster parents never implied that one of the reasons to accept Jesus was because He loved me, and I loved Him. It never occurred to me. I'm sure I wouldn't have understood much about love at that time in my life anyway.

I did manage to capture a boyfriend from church with my smile. I always had to sit by a window to keep from feeling trapped. One day after school, I was sitting on the bus looking out the window when I saw one of the Stecker boys who attended our church. He was older and always referred to me as a punkie freshman. His blond hair was tousled about. The first time, he just looked at me and smiled. The next time I saw him we began to talk. He treated me as if I were special. He bought me a white chocolate bunny and called me a few times a week during my ten-minute allotted phone time. He spoke with a heavy Jersey accent, so I called him Jersey Boy.

Church youth trips became our special time. We talked and laughed on the way. On one trip, we traveled to Mount Katahdin, the highest mountain in Maine at 5,268 feet. The name Katahdin means "greatest mountain." I was determined that I would conquer this great mountain. I was younger than the majority of the youth group. The older boys taunted us. "You will never make it! You will run out of water. There's no bathroom. You will have to go in in the woods. There are bears in the woods, big black bears." I was the only girl on that trip to make it to the top. Years later, I revisited that day with a one of the older boys on the trip who made the climb with me. He said, "When you made it to the top of that mountain you had arrived and we all knew it." I smiled and nodded.

I was very emotional during this period. I went through my freshman year at school with Ginny and my boyfriend, and my choices kept me constantly grounded. I often felt like a prisoner and, from time to time, would run away. I would drop to the ground from my second-floor window, but I never stayed gone long. I needed my mediator, Michael, to help me maintain some degree of self-esteem and pull me together when I felt lost. I just wanted to be free, and I thought I could somehow run away from my memories.

One early morning when I was sixteen, I dropped out of my bedroom window for the last time on Carver Road. I landed on the soft, wet grass, barely missing the vegetable garden we had planted earlier that spring. I passed under the weeping willow where Sissy and I played. I looked over my shoulder at the apple tree Sissy and I dreamed in. I couldn't allow myself time to think about leaving Sissy; otherwise, I wouldn't have left. I knew she was okay now. Mom favored her.

I had been formed here, carved into who I was now. I was alive now and like Pinocchio, ready to run away from the workshop. I thought of my room with daisy wallpaper. The white shelf over my bed filled with dolls, trophies from gymnastic competitions, piano recital certificates, a beaded purple tie, a rose from a boyfriend, and a promise ring.

The smell of the blooming lilacs grew fainter as I ran past the blue house across the road where my friends were still sleeping. In my purse was the charm bracelet I received from Mother years before. This was the only gift I remembered getting. During the years on Carver Road, Mom added charms to my charm bracelet: a piano, a graduation charm, a sweet-sixteen charm, and an amethyst birthstone. At the main road, I stuck out my thumb and caught a ride to Bangor.

5

FATHER AGAIN

I called Uncle Percy from the Bangor Mall, and he picked me up. I stayed with him for a short time. I didn't seem to fit there either. Uncle Percy was the spitting image of Mother and a hopeless drunk, but he was fun and I liked him. It wasn't long before he found out where my real father was and told me. It may be he was just trying to figure out a way to get me out of his house, and his refrigerator.

It had been ten years since I had seen or heard from Father and he was obviously curious and anxious to see me. He was living in California at the time, and if nothing else, I knew that going to visit him, even if for only a couple of weeks, would be a great way to get some revenge against Mother for breaking all the promises she made to me.

I dropped everything that was going on in my life at that moment. It was summertime so school was not a concern when I made the decision to leave for California. I really had hopes of finding someone I could belong to.

The State of Maine approved the trip, since I was legally their responsibility. I didn't get much resistance from my foster parents. In fact, it seemed as if they were actually glad to hear it.

When I arrived in California, Father, his wife, and five children were waiting. As he kissed my cheek, my stomach turned at the forgotten stench of alcohol and cigarettes. I eventually realized that only one of the children was actually his child; the rest were his wife's from a previous marriage. I somehow had the idea before I got there that I would be the center of Father's attention, but it was soon obvious he would have little opportunity for that. On the way home from the airport the children jumped all over the car and screamed at each other. They stared at me as if I were some kind of new animal at the zoo.

My two weeks came and went. They asked me to stay the remainder of the summer; they needed a babysitter. Father and his wife both worked, and there wasn't much between us in terms of a relationship.

Father drank all the time and there were lots of fights as a result. Sometimes he would be so drunk he would pass out on the floor, but not before making lewd comments to me, leaving me feeling unsafe. During one of these moments, I called Foster Mother and asked her if could come back home. I told her I just didn't want to be away from Sissy and out of touch with Michael and my friends. Mom's reply was, "I didn't pay for you to get there, and I'm not going to pay for you to get back." I felt trapped.

I had that familiar alone feeling again. I thought of my foster family and Sissy. Tears filled my eyes. I felt the pain of being rejected and abandoned by people who called themselves my family for the last time. I found a bottle of Valium in the bathroom and decided to take a couple to see if they would help me calm down. Before it was over, I had taken all of them in an attempt to kill that empty feeling inside. In the process, I almost ended it all.

I awoke in the hospital. I didn't want to wake up because I knew nothing had changed. I was still in California, still away from Sissy, and still away from Michael and my friends. I wanted to be the one leaving for a change, and the pills were a way to do that.

Soon after going home from the hospital, Father separated from his wife. I had the choice of living with Father in a hotel room or living with Father's mother-in-law who lived in a one-bedroom house behind them. I decided to live with this lady called Granny. I helped her cook and clean and attended school.

Granny was very demanding and very unappreciative of anything I did for her. Her laundry had to be walked to a Laundromat where I would go to wash, dry, and fold everything, then bring it back and put it away. My study time was a low priority for her.

I had just turned seventeen years old and the orphanage was beginning to look good to me compared to this experience. At least there I had Sissy and Pinocchio. During this time, Granny's twenty-seven-year-old son had moved in with her. This immediately doubled my workload and left no time for anything else. Her son found me attractive and talked about taking care of me. Anyone who said those words to me at that time in my life would have had my undying gratitude.

By this time, Father had disappeared again. He had abandoned me for the second time in a place where I knew no one except the strangers I lived with.

6

GAINING STRENGTH

At seventeen, I found myself pregnant. My foster parents didn't want me, so I felt like the only right thing to do was to get married and have a family. My life experience would never allow me the option of aborting this child, even though I wasn't sure if a permanent relationship with this man was anything I wanted. We married.

On December 16, 1976, I gave birth to my beautiful little daughter, Jamie Lynn. She was wrapped tightly in a pink blanket and placed in my arms. Through my tears, I kissed her sweet face and touched her tiny hand. I got a peek at her emerald eyes and smiled. I thought, *She is Beauty and Love and she is mine*. I was excited about the possibility of finally having someone no one could take away. Unlike Pinocchio, this child was mine, and I was hers. I needed her, and I was sure she needed me.

According to my husband, finishing school was not important. He wanted me to quit so that I could devote all my time to serving him and raising the baby.

Four years later on June 19, 1980, I had my second child, Paul Joseph. He was placed in my arms wrapped in a blue blanket. I kissed his sweet face and thought, *He is the most beautiful baby boy I have ever seen*. His eyes were just as brilliant as his sister's—emerald green and perfect.

My children were my life. As time passed, I became very

busy and submissive to my husband. I was convinced I had no right to play any kind of role in life other than the one my husband told me to have. I thought this was a normal life for two parents raising two children.

I was not allowed to wear shorts or learn how to drive. My husband always overrode my opinions and feelings about naming our children and other significant issues. I was his possession. Before long, I realized this was just another form imprisonment in a world over which I had no control. I had very little contact with anyone from my past during these years and focused all my attention on raising two precious children. I loved being their mother.

Because of my husband's concern about the California school system, and raising children there, we moved from California to Oklahoma where my husband had relatives. This became our new home.

In Oklahoma, I met Rhonda. Rhonda was a beautiful girl with bright blue eyes and long, blond hair. Rhonda was a strong, independent Texas girl who could stand toe to toe with a man and put up a good fight. She was shocked that I didn't wear makeup and couldn't drive. She taught me to drive a car while my husband was at work. At twenty-one, I had my very own Oklahoma driver's license. It didn't do me much good at first because my husband would not let me drive his car, license or not.

Rhonda had heard about a job at a nearby dollar store and told me I should apply. I was nervous, but excited. On my first interview, I was hired on the spot. I enjoyed working and being needed by my employer. I advanced through the ranks quickly and eventually ended up as part of the office staff, learning payroll and balancing money for bank deposits.

Rhonda watched the children while I worked and, for the first time, I was saving my own money. This was very good for my self-confidence. Before long, I found myself taking courses in order to complete my education, and I purchased my very own car. I was gradually gaining independence. It felt good to have a little control.

I was starting to experience this word *freedom* I had always heard people talk about.

Not long after my first car and my first job, my husband came home and told me he did not love me anymore. I was devastated and didn't know what to do. I tried to make things work, but even my best efforts weren't good enough. Years later we divorced. The marriage had lasted nine years. I found myself alone raising two children and working full time. I was, and am, grateful for my children. We had never spent a week separated from each other.

I dreaded telling anyone about the divorce. I especially avoided letting my foster parents know. I knew better than to call and ask them if I could bring my children with me back to Maine and live with them until I got back on my feet. I just knew I would have to make it on my own. I was determined. With a car, a job, and an education, I could do this.

7

CRUCIBLE

In January 1986, my children and I moved into a duplex in Moore, Oklahoma. I worked at a bank making just enough to make ends meet. I enrolled my children in school and was available to my children every day after school. We formed a new routine. The children played, I prepared supper, and they set the table. We held hands and prayed before each meal. We talked about our day, scurried through homework, and then teeth brushed and into jammies. "Hurry!" I would say, so we could snuggle on the couch under a warm blanket, play board games, or watch TV. It didn't matter; it was our special time. Then it was off to bed where they were tucked in tight, smothered with kisses, and I read them *Goodnight Moon*. I would then slide into a warm bath and disappear into weightless clouds of bubbles, surrounded by the smell of a lilac candle and the escape of Gregorian chants. In the middle of this peace, I felt an old familiar pain return.

While I was still going through my divorce, I met my second husband. He would come to my teller window at the bank at least once a week to make deposits. He appeared successful and always treated me with a certain reverence and respect. I was about to fall into that same trap baited with the illusion of security.

Within six months, we were married. We had a charming little wedding and a dream honeymoon in Hawaii. Soon, however, things began to change.

I had the opportunity to change careers and move into the medical field. I became an administrative assistant for a psychiatrist. I had always been motivated by a challenge. This led to a corporate management position for a national dental company. It came naturally for me to hide behind a pinstriped suit with a tight ponytail and manicured nails. At home, I transformed into normalcy. Church, children, and taking care of our home was my second job.

I ignored the warning signs of a crack opening in my soul. Memories of the past began to consume me. I was a little girl again scarred by shame and betrayal, lost in a forest thick enough to trap me. My marriage was crippled with stress, financial issues, a blended family, ex-spouses, and high tempers. We attended couples therapy briefly at our church with little result.

I began to feel trapped in a situation I could not escape. I struggled to swallow and couldn't breathe. My hands tingled with the burn of a thousand pins. My heartbeat felt like thunder and lightning. Pain spread down my legs. I was diagnosed with situational panic attacks and given medication to take at the onset. I declined them.

The simple joys of life became overshadowed by a sense of impending doom, breaking down twenty-seven years' work in building battlements to protect me. My will to fight was gone. I was exhausted by internal and external battles that simply didn't stop. Loneliness, abandonment, betrayal, failure, childhood, and marriage all cut through the core of my being like a saw to wood. I knew at that moment who my torturer was—Mother Betrayer. The doors burst open exposing pain as intense as labor. Revenge, hate, anger, and loss built to a crescendo. I picked up the phone and dialed Mother's phone number. When she answered, I just shouted, "I hate you!" and hung up. I slowly stopped having any contact with Sissy or my foster brothers and sisters because I just didn't want anyone to know how unhappy I was. I took a bottle of pills. I had determined that no one would leave me again. This time, I was going to be doing the leaving.

I woke the next morning confused and physically exhausted. I looked into the tearful eyes of my daughter. I saw an all-too-familiar pain as she gently held my hand. Her sweet, beautiful face desperately searched mine for answers. I realized with clarity I would do whatever it took to never attempt to silence or hurt myself again. I made her that promise. She saved my life.

HEALING

I was broken but not defeated. God met me right where I was. He was my Father *and* Mother. I read His word and prayerfully sought His will for my life. The very next Sunday I went forward for prayer during church. I prayed like I had never prayed before.

I decided to seek more counseling to finish the process of healing the child in me. I invested a significant amount of time that year consulting with a clinical psychologist. It was a frightening and painful process.

This was a time when I was forced to stop and face many critical issues impacting my life. I needed to forgive that little orphan girl inside me and begin to love and respect her rather than always find fault in her. Little did I know what this new beginning would bring. I finally stopped hating her and decided immediately to let her live. I was determined to have a future and realized only I could set the course.

Many things in my past resurfaced during my treatments, and many things did not. I found I was beginning to open up little by little. As I did, people around me responded to me differently. I learned many truths during this period of my life, one being that it's hard to have a friend if you're unwilling to be a friend.

God has placed very special people in my life at just the right times, and I finally realized I have really never been left alone. Several people came to encourage and support my renewed dedication to personal growth. One of them was a very special young lady where I worked. She played the role of sister from the very first time we met. I shared many of my deepest, personal feelings and circumstances with her along the way, and criticism or faultfinding never came from her. She always really listened and cared.

It was a refreshing new realization for me not to be raked over the coals every time I made a mistake. What a great revelation to learn that mistakes are necessary in order for us to grow. I owe an eternal debt of gratitude to the special angel God put in my life at that time, for believing in me, even before I believed in myself.

It was also during this time that my foster brother, Michael, came back into the picture. He had always been my great defender and never wavered in his strong belief in me as a person. He was now experiencing problems of his own and reached out to me for reassurance. He couldn't have known how much I needed him to call.

I found myself yearning for Sissy during this time, and as the healing of many of the deep-seated scars began to take place, I found that, one by one, the people I held dear in my life began to reappear. My world was beginning to look different in a wonderful kind of way each morning, and I felt a new excitement for living I had never known before. I began to feel this little pitiful girl inside evolve into a beautiful little princess who had life's circumstances as her duty bond subjects to rule and reign over. I had a constant daily battle between my old self and the new self I was determined to be. Some days I lost the battle, but most days I won. On bad days, I would just bury myself in doing things for my children and somehow find value in myself through that.

I still knew something was missing. I just didn't know what it was, or where to look for it. I prayed daily the desires of my heart, that God would be with me as I ventured out in search of the answer to this void.

Since the orphanage, I had thought about being free. I would envision myself walking on a sunny, sandy beach; wandering through a field of flowers that went on for as far as I could see; and hearing the sound of a warm breeze whipping through my hair. This vision had a way of making me feel peaceful and quietly content. That feeling is what I was searching for when I wasn't dreaming or in a momentary trance.

Occasionally, I would become frustrated and impatient with myself. The therapy, my children, and Michael, were my protection.

I recall a very special little card that Michael had given me, which I kept in my purse. I often would pull it out in the middle of a battle with myself and read the words: "I Love You Just Because You Are You." Those words seemed to work magic when I had my little relapses.

This miracle healing process that God had begun resulted in a renewed breath of life in all my relationships with loved ones. I realized if I didn't grow to love and respect myself, no one else would.

8

ANGELS

Beautiful days came. I was changing. I could tell because my attitude toward my life's circumstances underwent a significant adjustment. I could more easily find the good in situations, and I often would comment on the lesson I learned. I was gradually coming to terms with that little girl inside who I had persecuted all my life because I thought she deserved it. I began to love that little person who did not ask for any of what life had dealt her.

I was a kind and compassionate person. God had been merciful to me on many occasions and had always put the right people at the right time in my path to guide me to the next plateau on this quest.

One evening I answered the telephone and to my surprise found a voice from my past had found her way back into my life. My precious friend Ginny was on the other end of the line. I absolutely could not believe I was talking to her. Her voice was like a warm, gentle breeze soothing my soul.

We talked for hours that evening, catching up on twenty years of being apart. My heart warmed at the sound of Ginny's voice. Ginny and her husband owned a bed and breakfast in Booth Bay Harbor, near the Atlantic coast. For the first time in many years, I had a desire to go back home to Maine to see my school friend. We called each other at least once a week, and the more we talked, the more I wanted to see her. We exchanged pictures of our families, and soon I determined I needed to go back home and spend a week with her. She still lived in the general area where we grew up, so I would be able to visit my foster parents and my brother Brian while I was there.

I called my foster parents to let them know when I would be there. Foster Mother responded as if it might be an inconvenience, but ended with, "That's nice, dear" and "Yes, we would like to see you." I was disappointed in her response and considered canceling my plans.

While waiting for my trip to Maine, I began to wonder about my little brother, Robbie, and my little sister, Kelly. I had an old newspaper clipping from a previous trip to Maine that had Kelly's engagement announcement in it. I carried it in my Bible for several years, wondering if I should attempt to reach her. I had so many concerns. Honestly, I didn't think enough of myself before now to believe they would have any reason to want to know me, even if I did successfully reach them. The slow process of rebuilding my self-esteem and finding self-acceptance had given me the idea that maybe my brother and sister would really like to know how I was doing, or at least that I thought of them. I had always longed to be reunited with them, but twenty-seven years is a long time. Things change, and so do people.

During this time, I did two things that were instrumental in helping me take action. 1) I wrote down my greatest desire—to see my babies again. It was December 31, 1992, when I wrote that note. As I did, I said a silent prayer to God to help me make it happen; 2) I moved Kelly's announcement from my Bible to my wallet, so I could see it every time I opened my wallet.

One evening after work, I found myself alone in my quiet house. I sat down to balance my checkbook when I came across Kelly's picture on her wedding announcement. The next thing I knew, I was on the phone calling information for Kelly's number. When the operator asked me to hold for the number, I had a major explosion of adrenalin at the thought of actually having my sister's number. My mouth went dry. I could hardly catch my breath. I dialed the number and a man answered. I asked if Kelly was there. He said, "No, she is on vacation. I'm her dad; can I help you?" He had such gentle warmth in his voice, and I felt safe in telling him I was Lynnann, Kelly's sister. I told him I lived in Oklahoma and that I was planning a trip back to Maine and would just love to see her. Her father assured me that both Kelly and Robbie knew they were adopted and that they had a brother and two sisters out there.

I will never forget the words that followed. He said, "I don't see any reason at all why you all should not get together." He took all my flight information and kindly told me he would see to it that Kelly got the message as soon as she returned. He was expecting her to be back that evening. I thanked him for being so kind. I thank God that this man's warm and gentle voice was the one I heard on that incredible day in my life.

When I hung up the phone, I put my hands over my face and began to sob. I had just made the most important phone call of my life. My son asked me what was wrong, and I quietly told him I needed to pray. I went into my bedroom, got on my knees, and thanked God for giving me the strength and the courage to make that call. I thanked God for the kind person He placed there to receive my call. I had asked for my prayer on New Year's Eve just three months earlier to be answered—to contact Robbie and Kelly.

I knew at that point it could actually happen! I was higher than I had ever been in my life. I knew God was at work, perfecting one of the biggest miracles I could ever imagine.

9

ROBBIE

A couple of hours passed, and then the telephone rang. My son answered. He came into my room to tell me it was for me. He said, "It's your brother, Robbie!" I was so overcome with joy I just knew I would die before I got to the phone. I made it alive and picked up the phone.

What do you say to your brother after twenty-seven years? The answer is just about anything you want to. I spoke first, saying, "Hello?" and my dear, sweet brother at the other end of the line in all his Yankee glory said, "Hi there, how are you?"

He told me he had memories of me, though very few, and that he had always been able to remember my name. As we talked, we both began to cry. He told me he wanted to see me very much but didn't know how Kelly would feel. He said she had no memory of our early beginnings and this, no doubt, would be a very emotional thing for her to come to terms with. He did not know if she would want to see me. I must admit it was painful to hear that, but I determined that even if Robbie was the only one who wanted to see me, it would be more than I ever dreamed could happen.

Robbie assured me that he would do his best to convince Kelly that she should at least meet me. He also said he would respect her feelings and protect her if she chose not to. I respected that, and loved him even more for it. We talked for over an hour that evening and could hardly bring ourselves to conclude our conversation.

We promised each other we would write each other and share pictures of our families and ourselves in the next few weeks. He told me, "Nothing short of death would keep me from seeing you."

I just could not believe I had just talked to my brother after twenty-seven years of separation and that he loved me just as if I had never been gone. He didn't care a thing about my past; he just loved me because I was me. I always yearned for unconditional love. For many years, I didn't know it existed. We said good-bye knowing we would be holding each other very soon.

ANTICIPATION

I had never been so excited about an event in my life as this. I knew this experience would change me forever. I shopped for little Oklahoma treasures to take to them. I never really worried whether Kelly would be there or not. I just had peace inside about it and knew the best thing would happen, whatever it was.

I wrote a letter to Robbie and Kelly, thanking their father for his kindness to me. I shared my deep-felt gratitude for the opportunity to be a part of their lives. Robbie and I called each other frequently during this time. One day, Robbie told me Kelly would be joining us for our little reunion. I was so excited I immediately called Ginny. She insisted we hold the reunion at her bed and breakfast in Booth Bay Harbor. She said she could video the event and preserve it for me forever.

Things were magically beginning to come together. The photos I received from Robbie were just precious. He was so handsome, and I was so proud of him. I could hardly believe this was happening. The days seemed to drag by. I was afraid I would somehow pass away before this blessed event could happen. If God could get me this close, He could get me the rest of the way with very little effort. Finally, the day came for me to leave for Maine.

I had also planned to visit the orphanage during this trip. I shared with my children the story of the orphanage and my having been forced to leave Pinocchio there when I left.

I boarded the plane and passed the time listening to a special song I wanted to share with the others, realizing that today, April 17, 1993, my dreams would come true.

10

REUNION

The plane took off from Oklahoma City on time and reached Chicago as scheduled. I easily made my connecting flight to Bangor, Maine. While on this flight, I met a lady named Patricia. She began visiting with me about her family and her sisters. This gave me a chance to share my story with her. She was so moved by it she sobbed. I believe she really understood the importance of this trip to me. I still wonder if she was an angel sent by God to help me through the rest of the trip.

After reaching Bangor, I had one more leg to Portland. I was beginning to tingle. I thought, *It will only be another hour before I meet Robbie, Kelly Jo, and my friend Ginny.*

The Portland airport was fogged in, so we were delayed. No flights were coming into or going out of Portland. We waited for hours for the fog to lift, but it never did. Fear came over me as I thought of Ginny waiting for me and not seeing me arrive. I felt that old childhood fear of being abandoned again in Bangor. I am so thankful that God placed Patricia on that trip with me to console and encourage me to stay calm. She was the greatest help, and a most wonderful companion. With Patricia's help, we made the final leg of the journey to Portland by bus. That two-hour ride was a very special time; I believe God used it to help prepare me for what was about to happen. Patricia let me know that as long as she was around I would not be alone. She would remain with me until I was safely delivered to Portland. We laughed, cried, and felt so fortunate to have crossed paths, even though it would only be for a short time. Miracles still surprise me.

I finally arrived in Portland. There was Ginny. I was overjoyed to see her again. She had not changed much since high school. Her blond hair was shorter now and bobbed around her pretty face. She had the same light blue eyes. We hugged. It was like we were sixteen again. I was exhausted, and she carried herself with ease collecting my luggage. We filled up the gas tank and set out on a one-hour drive to her home in Booth Bay Harbor.

Our conversation never stopped. It was a nuisance to have to take a breath; we had so much to catch up on. She wanted details of my life, and I wanted details of hers. She wanted to know how I felt about meeting Kelly and Robbie. I couldn't express in words how I felt. It seemed like that one-hour trip was only fifteen minutes.

My heart was pounding. I felt sure I was going to hyperventilate, as my breathing just kept getting faster and faster. In no time, Ginny said, "We're home!" I opened the car door and Ginny said, "Oh no you don't. I've got to get the camcorder set up first." I thought it would be worth another couple of minutes to have this event recorded so I could relive it over and over.

As I walked in the door, there they were, coming down the stairway to meet me. I dropped my purse and went straight to Kelly. When our eyes met, I knew I was really home and the joy of this experience was only just beginning. I hugged her with both arms and felt my knees start to tremble. I began to cry. I held her at arm's length to look at her. She was no longer a baby. She was a young woman with brown eyes flecked with gold. Her long, red hair fell to her strong shoulders. She was equal parts Mother and Father.

I then turned to Robbie and embraced him with all the strength I had left in me. Robbie stood there with his broad Sepcich shoulders, his light brown hair tousled by the ball cap he held in his hand. His teeth were perfect and his olive skin unblemished. I was amazed. They were so perfect, so grown up, but to me they were still my little babies. I just couldn't stop shaking my head in disbelief that

I was actually having this incredible experience.

Ginny shut the camcorder off and we went to the kitchen and began talking as if we'd never been apart. I shared my memories of them as children, and we swapped pictures of each other and of our families. Ginny was constantly recording; I cannot begin to say how grateful I am for the treasure of film. Its value is priceless to my family and me.

We drank coffee and ate some of Ginny's famous rum balls as we sat at the kitchen table reminiscing. When Ginny and her husband went to prepare our rooms, we just stared at each other, asking, "Where have you been all my life?"

We spent that evening getting the ugly past out into the open. Kelly asked, "How could any mother just give up her kids? We were all so cute; why would anyone just give us away?" She had no memory of any of it but knew she was just a baby. I told her she was very fortunate the way things turned out. I knew in my heart that my little Kelly was going to be just fine. I had been concerned that my return into their lives would bring back horrid memories of things they may have suppressed. My memories were bad enough, and I had hopes that they wouldn't experience pain, but rather pleasure as a result of our getting back together.

I could see a lot of pain in Robbie's eyes as we revisited those early days of our lives—being locked in the car at Mother's bar or when I would call one of her boyfriends by name. He was old enough at the time to remember some of it. His eyes revealed not just pain, but a genuine compassion for the lady who sat across the table from him. He was grateful I had brought my life's journey full circle back to this table where he and I sat, sharing the experience with each other. I had finally managed to put together two pieces of a beautiful puzzle. I saw in Robbie a very special love for me, and I knew that he also was going to be just fine. We all were.

We finally decided to call it a day and headed to our rooms. Kelly said, "You can sleep with me tonight if you want to." I said, "I would love to." We kicked Robbie out for a couple of minutes while we dressed for bed. I had brought with me two long satin gowns; I gave Kelly the pink one and I wore the white one. I also brought a picture of the five of us when we were little, before we were all separated. There we were, our five little faces in front of a Christmas tree. It was the only picture I knew of with all five of us. I had it enlarged to a 5" x 7" size and put in five identical frames. I was on a mission to deliver one to each of my brothers and sisters this trip. This was the time to give Kelly and Robbie theirs.

When Robbie came back into the room, I presented him his first. His eyes filled with tears. He said, "Those five little faces—just look at those five little faces." Then I gave Kelly hers. She just stared at it speechlessly. The complete silence seemed to last a long time. I knew Kelly had absolutely no memory of that day. I broke the silence and said, "No one will ever keep us apart again. Those five little faces are in complete control of where we go from here. I will never let you two out of my life again now that I have you back. We are going to make it!" Kelly gave a peaceful smile and nodded.

Robbie went on to bed, and Kelly and I stayed up comparing our hands, toes, and legs. We swapped stories of our experiences at childbirth. Our lives were amazingly similar. We each had a boy and a girl. We both had worn braces, we both had been cheerleaders in school, and we seemed to share the ability to be sensitive to other's feelings.

We most certainly were sisters, having so many things in common. It was difficult to settle into sleep, but we finally did. I didn't fall asleep before I noticed she slept with one leg outside the covers, just like I do.

THE WALK

The morning was new and glorious. My reunion with Robbie and Kelly seemed to add another degree of intensity to the gold light of the morning sun. I had two incredible new reasons for greeting this particular day. The dawn of this day brought with it a renewed sense of purpose for me.

The three of us walked along the coast, rocks hand in hand, talking, laughing, and crying practically at the same time. This morning felt like a sample of the vision I had seen as a child where I was walking along the ocean with my family, feeling the breeze blowing through my hair. I looked at my long lost brother and sister and realized that for the first time in my life, I felt free. I felt complete. I had been transformed almost overnight into a truly new person. We took pictures of each other while enjoying the early morning quiet and eventually headed back to Ginny's place. We made plans to pack up and spend a couple of days in Guilford with Robbie's and Kelly's families.

The drive to Guilford gave us a chance to talk and plan the day. I was going to meet Robbie and Kelly's parents, those wonderful people who accepted the responsibility of raising and loving these two very special people of mine. We planned to have an evening meal at Kelly's house. I would meet her husband, Bob, and her two children, Erin Jo and JR. I would also meet Robbie's wife, Lisa, and their little boy, Ian. As we talked and drove, we began to open up to each other more and more. Kelly shared with me things that only sisters would share. I felt so very fortunate that she felt the freedom to share these deep secrets with me.

We arrived in Guilford right on schedule and standing at the front door of Kelly's house was her husband who greeted me with the most wonderful welcome hug. It was sweet. About that moment, I felt this little hand touch mine and as I looked down it was Kelly's little girl, Erin Jo. I reached down to kiss her. She looked just like I remember Kelly when I had last seen her so many years ago. I fell in love with her instantly. She handed me a precious little card she had made for me. She told me she had spent the day preparing for my arrival, styling her hair and making the card.

Then came little JR. This little boy was a firecracker in the flesh. At fifteen months old, he flew from one room to another. He and Erin Jo had a very strong resemblance. The picture of them jolted my memory back twenty-seven years in an instant, recalling those difficult days at their age.

Next, I met Robbie's wife, Lisa, and their son, Ian. They had all agreed to meet at Kelly's house. Lisa was full of life and kept everything moving. Ian was simply adorable. He called me Auntie and loved it when I took his picture. He seemed to enjoy giving me a big kiss right on the lips. After Ian got a few good "sugars," JR decided he was not to be out done and planted a few good ones on me too.

When I was introduced to Robbie and Kelly's parents, it was very clear to me how they felt about my being there. Their father gave me a big hug and smile, and said, "Welcome, dear." Their mother also hugged me and welcomed me. They brought out Kelly's and Robbie's photo albums. What a joy to see! Those albums answered so many of my questions. After a time of reminiscing, we all sat down to eat, and I briefly wondered what might have been had these kind people been my mom and dad too.

I felt a deep sense of gratitude for what these two wonderful people had done so unselfishly for Kelly and Robbie, and I knew that we had the common bond of sharing in the survival and triumph of these most precious people, my brother and sister. They were Robbie and Kelly's source of love, security, food, clothing, shelter, and so much more. They gave them something that a foster family just could not give me—a solid sense of self. We shared a common bond—a love for my brother and sister. I was so grateful for them at that moment.

After our meal, we went through the photo albums. Some of the pictures brought back the very memories I had kept in a place of honor, fighting never to forget those faces as long as I lived. Faces that had been taken away from me. I was overwhelmed and had to leave the room a couple of times to regain my composure. Later on, their dad joked with me about my Oklahoma accent. We all had a great time.

That evening just flew by. I met Bob's mother who, when I

reached out to shake her hand, asked if she could give me a hug. I had never been hugged and kissed more in my life than that night. I felt loved and a part of this beautiful family. I met Bob's sister, who was also very sweet. They all seemed to stare at me now and then. Finally, Bob said, "Sweetheart, I know you think I'm staring, but I just can't help it; you look just like my wife!"

I was warmed by the love that all these people felt for me and generously showed me. Kelly and Robbie's parents invited my family and me to return in the summer and stay at the family cabin! As they prepared to leave, I insisted on taking some more pictures of them.

I felt such a strong sense of attachment to them. I could not bear for them to leave. I had to slip off to the bathroom and cry at one point. When I came out, Bob was there with one of his big hugs to help me find the strength to say good-bye to them. Their dad hugged and kissed me on the top of my head and said, "I'd have taken all five of you children if I could have." I almost collapsed as those words penetrated my being. I never had a parent figure say they really wanted me. These people have a very special place in my heart, set aside just for them. What a day this had been! How could one person experience so much in one twenty-four-hour period?

Robbie said his goodnights and went home with the anticipation of a new day. Kelly's husband, Bob, soon found out that he would be spending the night in the children's room because, yeah, Kelly and I got the master bedroom. We put on our satin nighties and called it a day.

We awoke the next morning to the phone ringing. It was Robbie saying, "Get up! I'm coming!" The plan for the day was that Kelly would go to work, and Robbie and I were going to hit the road and cover some ground together driving to Bangor to the orphanage and then on to Hampden where my foster parents lived. We would then return to Guilford where I would prepare a meal for my babies. I needed to do that. I had to feed them. They were always so hungry when we were little. I knew I wanted our last night there to be a celebration, a happy time together with plenty of love and food.

When Robbie arrived that morning, Kelly and I were still sitting at the table having our morning coffee. I was giving Kelly a manicure and a pedicure before we took our showers. We had just decided we'd better get in gear when Bubba arrived. Kelly, Erin, and I all crowded into the bathroom and got prissed up for the day. We said our so-longs and looked forward to our great celebration later that evening.

Robbie and I headed out. It was a wonderful time together. We talked at times and at other times, we just shared a glance or a smile. Words were unnecessary. Robbie would reach out his hand to mine, and I would feel so proud of this brother of mine who had grown into such a handsome young man. I told him how proud I was of him and his beautiful family. I shared how good it felt to know that he played the role of protector for Kelly over the years. I somehow felt safe and secure with Robbie. I loved feeling safe again.

When we arrived in Bangor, my heart began to race as we drove up the long, lonesome driveway to the front door. We got out of the car and saw that the orphanage was now used as a day care center. It was closed that particular day. Robbie and I walked around the building, and I shared with him some of the memories I had of this place.

I tried all the doors and found them locked. The irony struck me—all those years I tried so desperately to escape this place and here I was trying hard to get in. As we circled the building, I pointed out the window to the room where I was disciplined. I began to weep uncontrollably. I could feel the presence of the little girl I left there. I wanted in to rescue her. As the tears came, I felt Robbie's strong arms around me and his quiet, gentle voice saying, "Let it out, baby, let it all out." I felt as if I were that little girl again trapped in this prison, when Robbie tugged me back to the reality of the moment, reminding me I had a whole new family now, that I was a wonderful person, and that so many people loved and needed me. He reminded me that I am someone's sister, Ian's auntie, and that everything would be okay.

Robbie was my lifeline back to the present, preventing the memory of this place and the past from swallowing me up and taking me away from them all over again. He was my protector, defending me against old feelings of loneliness and abandonment, battling with me for the personal dignity I knew I had a right to. I knew he would love and protect me from now on.

We prepared to leave, and a sense of quiet contentment came over me. It felt good. As we drove away, I looked back at the orphanage and said to myself, "Tomorrow I'll be back."

Our next stop was to be Brian's place. Robbie and I had both been in touch with Brian, but this was our first occasion to see him together. Brian and I were older than the others and had the strongest memories of the worst times. This created a strong bond between us, so strong we never needed to speak about them. We knew the truth when our eyes met. We had always been silent about the past. On this day, I did not know what to expect from Brian.

We lost contact after the orphanage, until at seventeen when I went to see Father. Brian was in the navy and came to see me there. We were all walking on the beach one day, and Father was drunk. He said something disrespectful to me and Brian knocked him out with one punch. He was still so full of anger. One thing was certain—he loved me.

Brian was the one who had tried to maintain a relationship with Mother over the years. He was so desperate for a mother's love that he subjected himself to her continued verbal abuse into his adult life. When he had enough rejection from her, he would always call me for acceptance and love.

We pulled into the drive and Brian stepped outside as we drove up. He was so handsome to me. His blond hair fell across his forehead. Hints of red showed in his thick, blond moustache. His strength was visible in his broad shoulders and easy stride. I got out of the car and gave him a big hug and kiss. I could tell he was hurting inside by the look in his brown eyes. We were alone for a few minutes.

"Brian, no one could ever take the place of my big brother.

I love you so very much. I want you to know that I would never intentionally hurt you. I want you to get to know Kelly and Robbie as I have."

"I'm proud of you, Sis. Nothing stopped you. You were the one to do this." He began to relax and enjoy our visit.

Brian's wife was home and she took pictures of the three of us as we spent a joyous time together. I presented to Brian his picture of "those five little faces" and witnessed the emotion as it overcame him. He asked, "Where in the world did you get this?" as tears streamed down his face. My heart broke to see him battle with the pain of being apart from his brothers and sisters for so many years. I knew the pain he felt, and I knew it hurt a lot.

He stood up and said, "I want to show you something, Sis." He dropped his Levi's and stood there in his boxers. I saw the horrible white scar from his thigh to just below his knee. I stared, my mind racing back to the little house in Louisiana, the screeching sound of tires, the small closet we hid in, the opening of the screen door, and the fear I felt. "Do you remember this?"

"Yes, I do."

"I remember it every day of my life."

"I know, Brother, I'm so sorry."

He pulled up his jeans and sat down. I reached over and patted his leg. He was tearful. We sat in silence.

We ended our visit with promises of getting together in August, and my reassurance to Brian that I would never be more than a phone call away if he wanted to talk with me. I wanted him to know that I would be praying for him to find peace in his heart. I suggested that he consider visiting with someone who could help him sort out his the feelings. We hugged again, and I silently prayed for him.

Robbie and I headed for our next stop—my foster parent's house in Hampden. We stayed about an hour. I told them I would like to come back the next evening and make them dinner. Mom informed me that they had a wedding shower to attend that night and that I should make it a little earlier in order to give them time to get ready. I felt a bit of the power struggle she and I shared over Sissy. Our eyes met in silence. This time, I didn't rebel. I knew that if I had to put them in a position to decide whether to have a meal with me or go to a wedding shower, I would be at great risk of being a lower priority. So to be safe, I said I would return the next afternoon instead.

Robbie and I were on our way out to leave when one of my foster sisters came in the door. She did not have a single word to say as we passed each other, until I said, "Hello, how are you?" She said, "Hi" and never looked back. I knew then I was home for sure.

From top left to right, Karen, Kelly, Brian, Robbie, Lynnann

On our way back to Guilford, Robbie and I reflected on the day's events. He said he was astounded at the total lack of emotion in my foster parents' greeting. He wondered why I continued to bother trying to keep that kind of relationship alive. Robbie was beginning to get a glimpse of what I had experienced in his absence during my years at the orphanage and in the foster home. He had pain in his eyes as he talked about it. That protective side showed itself again as he reassured me of how lucky he felt to have me as his sister and to have me back in his life.

Robbie is four years younger than I am, but he is an old soul. He and I were very much in tune with each other that day. I knew I was the lucky one. As we rolled the miles beneath us, we discovered a common appreciation for a loud radio and classic rock-and-roll music. We jammed all the way back, interrupted only by one more film stop.

CELEBRATION

After arriving back at Kelly's house, I changed into jeans, and a Maine sweatshirt that belonged to Bob. I put my hair in a bow and got to work. Kelly and Bob had not yet arrived home from work, but Lisa and Robbie were ready to help me get things ready. We hoped we would have everything done by the time they got home. I put Robbie to work cutting peppers and onions. Lisa set the table, and we prepared for our evening celebration meal. We took plenty of pictures and passed out lots of hugs during the preparation of the meal. My famous spaghetti sauce was ready. Bob and Kelly arrived right on cue, just as everything was finished.

Kelly came straight to me and hugged me. She said, "I don't want this night to ever end." She began to cry. I took her in my arms and told her what I had told Robbie, "This night, we are celebrating life." I told her that even though this may be our last night in each other's presence for a while, we were going to have fun together and just have a party. We were celebrating the beginning of the rest of our lives together, rather than an end to the twenty-seven years we spent apart. The children were fed first and then the rest of us ate. I piled all my babies' plates high. I wanted them to eat until they just couldn't eat another bite.

After plenty of food and good conversation, we cleaned up and decided to go over to Robbie's house so Ian could take his bath and get ready for bed. It was heartwarming to watch Lisa and Robbie team up to get Ian ready for a good night's sleep. Robbie rocked Ian for a bit before bed while I looked at photo albums.

We weren't there long before the phone rang. It was Kelly wanting me to come back to her house. After Ian was safely tucked in, Robbie and I headed back to Kelly's. I had a very special time with Kelly's daughter, little Erin Jo as she was going to bed. I read her a bedtime story and prayed with her before she went off to sleep. I treasure the pictures and the memory of those moments with Erin.

Kelly and I sat at the dining room table and put highlights in her hair. The guys were in the kitchen too, talking, taking pictures, and playing with the camcorder. Scott, one of their very good friends from high school, came over that night. I thought he looked like a Skippy rather than Scott, so I decided to rename him Skippy for the evening. He was just what we needed to keep everything upbeat and fun. He kept us rolling all evening, and he helped keep our attention off the fact that I would be leaving in the morning.

I finished Kelly's hair and then gave her a facial. I decided she also needed a bow in her hair and some lipstick. When we finished, we giggled and pranced into the dining room to dazzle and confuse the boys with our resemblance. I bet Bob had nightmares for weeks of there being two Kellys. We had so much fun that night looking like each other. We even tried to do splits like we did as cheerleaders. We still had it!

I played the song for them that always lingered in the back of mind over the years: "Someday We'll Be Together" by Diana Ross. We held each other and danced. We were together at last.

Skippy went home and Robbie was next to leave. It was hard for him, but we promised we would see each other for at least a moment in the morning. Bob found what was beginning to become a familiar sleeping spot for him in the children's room, and Kelly and I went on to bed. We held each other and talked until two o'clock in the morning.

The next morning we all parted. This time, we all knew the farewells were temporary, and bearable. I reassured Robbie of my love for him and told him I felt so very honored to be a part of his life again. There were tears for both of us as he departed for work. He drove away waving. I didn't want him to go. A powerful force had brought us together, and the barriers placed between us over time by others were obliterated now. I told Erin Jo, Kelly's daughter, goodbye and kissed her. I reminded her to say her night prayers each night while I was gone. I kissed little JR and gave him his hug as Kelly and I headed out for Robbie's house. We had planned to meet Lisa and Ian and follow her to the site where we would meet up with

Ginny. As we started for the road, a wild man in a pick-up truck came flying down the road. It was Robbie! He jumped out of his truck and grabbed me completely off the ground for one more big hug, and he was gone almost as fast as he had gotten there.

Kelly, Bob, Lisa, and I headed out to where Ginny had planned to meet us. We all met in a parking lot—camcorders running—to say farewell for a while. Tears flowed and hugs were plentiful as we struggled to part from each other. Kelly showed Lisa and Ginny the highlights I had put in her hair the night before. She said, "Lynnann gave me a facial and did my finger and toe nails; we did all the 'sister' stuff in just two days!" We shared forty-eight hours together, and the love that binds sisters could not be denied. I had a sense of wholeness within that I had never felt before. My goodbyes to Bob and Lisa were difficult too. These people had accepted me unconditionally and without hesitation, and I will never forget our first days together. I thought, *Goodbye, my babies, I will see you soon.*

I felt a new level of courage and determination as I set out with Ginny to confront the orphanage again.

11

ESCAPING ASYLUM

I planned to spend the next few days with Ginny. Our journey took us straight to Bangor. I talked constantly about the last two days with Kelly and Robbie. I overflowed with emotion and a sense of who I was. We drove up to the orphanage, and today the door was open for business. This day would prove to be as incredible as the previous days.

Ginny took the camcorder and recorded me walking up to the front door. It was ominous to me, even as an adult. As I opened that big front door and entered, the first thing I saw was the office, the very same office we were taken to the first time we came to this place. The orphanage could still cause me to tremble, still looking so big on the outside, but curiously smaller on the inside. The stair rails weren't as tall, the ceilings weren't as high, the windows not as big, and the counters not as high. I walked into the office and asked if I could take a look around. A young lady in the office, Deirdre, said I was welcome to. She asked if I had spent time in the children's home in the past and had a genuine interest in who I was and why I was there. Her smile immediately made me feel more comfortable. I found my speech difficult as I tried to recount for her the time I had been there.

It hit me that I was actually in the children's home where I had been abandoned and had learned the meaning of lonely. I was standing in the very same spot I had stood as a frightened little girl, only this time I was a thirty-four-year-old woman. This time, I was not alone. I had my Creator with me, I had Ginny, and Dierdre, who listened to every word and breath, as if it meant life or death.

Dierdre gave me a pencil and piece of paper and asked me to write down the names and dates of the things I could remember. She wanted to know my date of birth and who my brothers and sisters were so she could attempt to find some of the records that might still be there. She said there were boxes of files in the attic that were left there after the building ceased to be a state-run children's home.

She was very happy to take me on a tour of the building. We walked into the dining room. The room still felt large, but the furniture looked shrunken. I sat down on the stairs I had cleaned every Saturday when I was seven years old and began to feel that lonesome, frightened feeling all over again.

It was at about that moment that Ginny asked Dierdre if by chance she had seen a little Pinocchio hand puppet laying around anywhere. I had shared my story with Ginny of how Pinocchio and I had been separated years earlier. I thought Dierdre had seen a ghost. The color faded from her face, and she immediately turned and ran out of the room, saying, "Oh my God, wait a minute!"

A few seconds later, she returned with my Pinocchio! She and Ginny kept asking, "Is this it, Lynnann, is this it?"

I was totally speechless. I had once again come face to face with my old friend from the past. I looked at Pinocchio, then at Ginny, and then Pinocchio until I could finally speak. I asked, "May I please take him home?"

Dierdre replied, "Oh my God, yes! Yes! You may have your Pinocchio puppet!"

We were all in tears by then. I put him on my hand and held him to my chest, not believing I really had him back. His little face still bore that kind, gentle smile. It was obvious why he had become my best friend while I was in this place. I never dreamed I would ever see him again, even though as a kid I vowed to come back for him one day.

Dierdre said that Pinocchio had been kept in a toy box full of other toys, which belonged to a lady who had worked there for the past twenty-five years. She happened to be off that particular day. My thoughts are with those children today who have never been reunited with their special toy in that old toy box. These toys do not belong to anyone but the children they were given to by Santa. I wish I could hand deliver each one of those toys to their rightful owners. I wonder if other orphans, like me, have gone through life thinking that anything they owned could be taken away from them at a moment's notice. This simple hand puppet on my hand represented far more than a Christmas gift marked "boy or girl." It was a trophy for having run the race, and finishing sane. I thank God for His mercy to me, and for the kindest reminder that He had always been by my side, even at my loneliest moment.

Dierdre continued our tour, first the main floor and then the second floor. Most of this area seemed unfamiliar to me, although those stairs were *very* familiar. After touring the first two floors, we came to some tall, dark-stained doors. Up to that, point Dierdre had been leading the way, showing all the rooms and asking me if I had any recollection of what she was showing me.

We entered the passageway going to the third level, and I suddenly began to recognize things. This part of the building was all too familiar. We topped the stairs, and Dierdre showed us one room and then we crossed to another large, empty room. I knew for sure that this had been my bedroom. I began to feel very sick as I walked into that room and across to the window. I would stand for hours watching cars go down the road, hoping one of them would stop and get me out of there.

After gazing out at that old familiar view, I turned to Ginny and Dierdre, and with tears in my eyes, said, "This is it; this is my room." When we left the room, I asked if I could lead the tour; I now knew the way to all the rooms and would share what happened in each of them as we went.

I led them to the playroom. I showed them where they locked up Pinocchio every day and explained how if I had been very good, I would get to play with him for thirty minutes. We then went to the room where the floor matron stayed. This big, cold room had a window overlooking the huge white Standpipe. This was the window where I would lose myself in my own thoughts while I was being disciplined and whipped. I had achieved the ability to totally block out everything that was happening to me, and around me, by focusing on the Standpipe outside that very window. To adults, I would often seem to be totally untouchable emotionally. As I would read later, I was characterized as someone who was beyond hope.

After leaving Floor Matron's room, we went to another large room that, at the time, was unfamiliar to me. It was only later when I shared my journey through the orphanage with Sissy that she reminded me that this was the room they used to lock me in whenever all else would fail, in order to discipline me. I had blocked it out of my mind completely until then. It makes sense to me now why even to this day I still am slightly claustrophobic.

The tour of the third floor was nearly complete when Dierdre asked, "Do you remember the bats?" Of course I did. The stairway to the attic opened up just outside what was my bedroom. Even though I have a horrible fear of bats, on this day, it could have been lions, tigers, or bears; they would not have stopped me from going on up into the attic. On any other day, you'd find me climbing on top of furniture at the mere mention of a mouse, but today, I had an unusual courage.

As we opened the attic door, I felt as if I had unlocked the last door to my past. This was where I would find myself. Boxes filled with records and file folders were scattered all over the place. I wandered from box to box looking for some remnant of history, not sure what I was looking for. When I saw the number of boxes of files, I had little hope of finding anything that would give me a glimpse of what had happened, and why we had ever been there.

In less than three minutes, Dierdre called out to us "Sepcich, Brian, Lynnann, Sissy, and Robert."

My first reaction was, "My God!" I was in absolute shock at finding this long lost truth. Dierdre cautioned me that she didn't know what might be contained in that file. I took it and held it close to my heart, clutching it as if it were the key to knowing the answers to a million questions.

I opened the file and began to read the contents, searching for answers. I found I was admitted to the Bangor Children's Home on September 1, 1966, along with Brian and Sissy. The next page was dated August 18, 1966. It was an interview with Mother. It stated that she had requested that the state take us, and that she attributed to the breakup of her marriage. In one paragraph, they described her as a person who appeared to be on the verge of a nervous breakdown. A few paragraphs later, they described her as "a neat-looking, young woman who appeared quite calm." It angered me to read that she had blamed those five little faces for her problems. We were the excuse she used to justify her behavior. I'm sure we were a bit inconvenient for the lifestyle she chose, but I don't remember one of us asking to be abandoned.

These records contained detailed information on Mother's and Father's dates of birth and their heritage. It also contained information about relatives and a detailed analysis of each child. Along with these documents, I found the applications Mother had filled out and signed, giving us up to the state. For years after she came back around, she told me she had nothing to do with us being taken away, that her mother, father, and others had conspired to take us away from her. I always knew she was lying, but until now, I lacked any proof. Today, I read it for myself, and in this dusty attic, I learned the whole truth about why I found myself in this terrible place.

I read about Brian aloud, and the words tore at my heart, opening my eyes to the torment he had to have borne. I learned more of who he had become. When I came to my description, I read aloud again. They described me as a "pale, thin, unattractive child." I just could not stop reading, paragraph after paragraph, and page after page. It seemed my teachers were quite discouraged with me. I began to grieve for that sweet little girl inside me. How could anyone have treated her like that? I needed to be loved, not judged, during this awful experience.

I finally understood why it seemed like I was there forever. I had been discharged on March 24, 1967, and then readmitted on July 26, 1967. I have no recollection of Mother ever visiting us. I confirmed that Mother had signed us over to the state not once, but twice, during this period. These dates were so important for me to know. It was as if I finally had a hold of something tangible about my past, rather than a mystery that always haunted me. It wasn't pretty, but it was the truth. I can deal with the truth. Here were the applications, the boarding agreements, and the consent forms signed by Mother for Brian, Sissy, and me.

My heart broke to read about how they described our physical condition on our second return to the home. It said that we were not in good health. We were committed to the State of Maine on grounds of desertion. My grandparents had stated they couldn't care for us and that Mother had left town without their knowledge. I had never felt wanted by Mother, or any of my relatives, and now I had the original documents to verify they did not.

I realized I had been reading for quite some time. We were all in tears, sitting quietly in the attic of this mammoth place. We finished the remainder of the tour, and Deirdre let me keep my file. Ginny and I walked out of the children's home quite different than we had walked in.

This place had a way of changing a person. This time, however, it was for the better. I walked out with answers rather than questions, and with my friends rather than alone. I found a way to rise above the policies of a state. I had been reunited with a little friend who, for twenty-five years, had never given up hope of my return and, judging by his smile, was obviously happy to see me. I felt as though I had been in a battle and had been the victor. Pinocchio was the flag I would wave for all the world to see, that this day I had conquered my greatest foes: low self-worth, lack of self-acceptance, loneliness, frustration with the questions *why?* and *why me?*, a feeling of emptiness, and insecurity. I finally had the answer to why I was always ready to strike back, or in some cases take flight, when someone hurt me. It showed me how I had come to feel responsible for every circumstance that anyone would encounter.

These pearls of understanding would not only serve me, but my children and my children's children for generations to come. It was this knowledge, and the grace of God, that would forever change our heritage, my destiny, and those I would influence. Ginny, Pinocchio, and I left that afternoon hand in hand, victors.

12

MAINE

Ginny and I continued our plan for me to spend time at my foster parents' house. After Ginny dropped me off, I asked if I might lie down for a little bit. My head was pounding from all the emotion I had just experienced. Mom seemed put out by my asking and acted as if I should feel fortunate to even have the privilege of being there. The negative things I had read earlier about me in those files made me emotionally sensitive. Sitting in this house was depressing.

Ginny finally arrived to pick me up. She could tell I was distressed and that my visit with my foster parents had been stressful. She listened and comforted me as I cried my heart out.

I had one more precious little face to give a picture to—Sissy, who had shared this ordeal with me for many of those years. I found Sissy home, looking beautiful and unusually happy with life. She had met a very special young man who treated her well. He brought out of Sissy the happy laughter that I so love to hear when I am around her. Maybe Sissy had just learned to be happy on her own, I don't know. I just know that it made me happy. We have always had a strong bond between us because of our experience together. We had an absolutely wonderful visit. We laughed, cried, and covered a lot of ground during our visit.

I took out the picture of those five little faces and gave it to Sissy. She was speechless. She was very appreciative and thought what I'd done with the picture was very sweet. As I shared with her the events of the previous few hours, and my discovery of the documents at the orphanage, she became very interested in getting a set for herself. I was fearful about how she would react to some of the information in the file, so I gave her a thumbnail sketch of it all. I suggested she go and get a copy for herself, but she begged me not to make her go to the orphanage to get them. I told her I would make her copies and send them after I got home. I shared with her what I shared with our brother Brian—respect the things that happened in the past and learn from it, but we have to live our lives in the present and stay focused on what we want now, not what we wanted then or what should have been. I told her that understanding how the past has formed and shaped our thinking could be such a powerful way to change the way we think. I told Sissy that she would have the key to many doors to the past and had a choice to use it to find inspiration and self-acceptance.

Sissy, like me, has had enough misery and self-defeating behavior for one lifetime. I was confident by the time I left that she would be fine with it all. Sissy and I parted that night closer than we had ever been. I had a deeper appreciation for the person she had become. Sissy is one of my heroes, a wonderful mother, a precious sister, and my best friend.

I came to Maine with four pictures and love to deliver. I would leave with that part of my mission fully realized. It was as if I had successfully moved a mountain. I have such a wonderful friend in Ginny. She coordinated my transportation to perfection and shared some of the most incredible moments of my life with me. I spent the remainder of my time in Maine focusing on Ginny and her family, learning how to bake bread, driving along the shoreline of the Atlantic, and just plain enjoying her special company.

I felt like there had been a battalion of angels sent from God to stand with me on this trip, and in my mind, Ginny was one of them. I'm not sure I would have survived all this without her constant support and encouragement.

13

THE LAST DOOR

The day for me to leave for Vermont to see Michael on my next to last leg of this quest had arrived. Ginny helped me pack and we left for the airport. In Portland, we ate at a quaint little restaurant on the coast, watched the waves beat the rocky shoreline, and shared the afterglow of this beautiful reunion. We talked and laughed until I missed my plane by a mere five minutes. Ginny pretended to be disappointed, but I could tell that inside she was shouting with glee.

I made arrangements to catch the next flight, and this time, I made it on the plane. Michael recently had his own share of disappointments and I knew he needed some encouragement. I thought I might cheer him up. He greeted me at the door with his usual big kiss and hug and made me feel so welcome. Michael has never changed in that way. He has certainly been one of the very good things that came out of my foster-home experience.

I shared with him the events of the previous several days. He watched the video Ginny had taken with great interest. He read every word of the file from the orphanage and even got a kiss from Pinocchio. Michael was very moved by it all, and even though he is a big, strong man, the tender side of him would show now and again, evidenced by a little trail of a tear.

Michael's childhood was much like mine, with the exception of his adoption by our foster parents. I asked him on our walk through the woods whether or not he ever wanted to know more about his childhood. He was adopted at age four and had no contact with his birth parents from then on. I told him I thought it would do him good just to be able to ask some of the questions I knew he must have about those days, and how it all happened. I told him that it didn't matter how his birth mother responded or what she said. He would find satisfaction in finding the courage to ask, and he would somehow get loose from any emotional bondage that he might have developed from unanswered questions.

I picked up pinecones and put them in my pockets as we strolled along on that glorious sunny day. Michael insisted that I had brought the sunshine with me. I responded by telling him that I would do anything I could to share with him the peace I felt in my heart at that moment. I felt the seed had been planted for Michael seriously to consider getting some answers of his own. When we parted after our visit, I left Michael with my love and a spot of hope that he would search for some of the missing pieces of his own life.

Approximately two weeks after my return from Vermont, on Mother's Day, my phone rang in the middle of the afternoon. It was Michael calling to tell me that he had called his birth mother and his biological sister. He asked questions and got answers. Like me, he found it wasn't all pretty, but it was the truth. Those familiar words, "The truth shall set you free" took on new meaning for both Michael and me. Michael made plans to see his biological sister in the near future. I was so proud of him for following through.

I will always hold dear the words he said to me that afternoon. For the first time, he told me that he needed me and wanted me in his life, that I had been what he came to believe family was all about. He was grateful for the encouragement I had given him to make that call. I collapsed on the bed after that call at the thought of having a story and an experience to share that, hopefully, would have a positive impact on another person's life. I hope that I can experience that opportunity many times over in the days and years ahead.

I escaped a bewildering forest of doors. Through the last door, I experienced a release from pain. I realized I was deserving of the love of others and myself. The labels *abandoned*, *orphaned*, and *foster child* dropped away, and I was simply me. I know who I am now. I know who I have become.

Twenty years ago, I left on an emotional and physical quest to rescue a hidden treasure—a little girl I left behind. I searched for the key to release her from prison. In a dark orphanage, I found her cowering and clutching her puppet. I unlocked the last door, dropped my sword, and took her by the hand. We walked into the light of my family's love.

THE BEGINNING

CPSIA information can be obtained at www.ICGtesting.com
Printed in the USA
LVOW13*0732081113

360321LV00004B/4/P